A Compilation of 11 Authors Emerging
TRIUMPHANT After Divorce

Divorced...

NOT

Devastated

Kimberly Perry Sanderlin

Divorced...NOT Devastated

Printed in the United States of America

Copyright @ 2018 Kimberly Perry Sanderlin

The copyright laws of the United States of America protect this book. No part of this publication may be reproduced or stored in a retrieval system for commercial gain or profit.

No part of this publication may be stored electronically or otherwise transmitted in any form or by any means- for example, electronic, photocopy, recording-without written permission of the author.

Scripture quotations are taken from the Holy Bible, New Living Translation, copyright © 1996, 2004, 2007, 2013, 2015 by Tyndale House Foundation. All rights reserved.

Book Coaching & Editing by:
SynergyEd Consulting/ www.synergyedconsulting.com

Cover Design & Marketing: Greenlight Creations
www.glightcreations.com/ glightcreations@gmail.com

Photography: In God's Image- Photographer Tanisha Walker
www.ingodsimage.net

Published by: SHERO PUBLISHING
SHEROPublishing.com / ericaperrygreen@gmail.com
For copies and publishing information, call 803-757-4376

Printing: Impress Print & Graphics Solutions
Library of Congress Cataloging-in-Publication Data

ISBN-13: 978-0-9994470-5-5

Be it advised that all information within this literary work, Divorced...NOT Devastated, has been acknowledged to be the truthful account of each author. The authors are responsible for the content in their individual chapter and hold Shero Publishing and SynergyEd Consulting harmless for any legal action arising as a result of their participation in this publication.

Table of Contents

Dedication	4
Acknowledgements	6
Foreward	10
Sleeping with the Enemy, *Kimberly Perry-Sanderlin*	12
Disappearing Acts, *Takiya Lewis*	40
From the Pauper to the Prince, *Natasha Perry*	52
If I Were to be Honest, *Tonza D. Ruffin*	68
The Preacher's Son, *Errico Moore*	82
Provoked Pain, *LaKesha Lakes*	100
Disillusionment, *Angela Brown*	118
Enough, *Janera Harvey*	134
The Detox is Real, *Ayanna Smith*	150
The Signs Were There, *Joan Sharpe McCullough*	162
12 Years a Slave, *Ebonie Aiken*	182

Dedication

This book is dedicated to every man and woman around the world who will read our journeys. It's dedicated to every person who is contemplating divorce, separated, going through divorce, or simply supporting women's journeys. Wherever you are on the spectrum, we hope *Divorced... NOT Devastated* helps you gain clarity, strength, and wisdom for the next step along your journey. We pray God's strength over you as you begin to walk into your destiny. And if that destiny includes the journey of "divorce," we pray that our journeys inspire you to boldly declare that you are *Divorced... NOT Devastated*!!

Blessings,

Kimberly Perry-Sanderlin

Divorced...NOT Devastated

When God placed this project in my heart in 2017, I honestly ran away from it! Divorce is not the usual conversation around the dinner table. In fact, though divorce is occurring at an increasingly alarming rate, it still remains taboo in 21st century society. This has been a spiritual journey, within all authors being drawn to the project within the first 72-hours of its inception! The DND team is excited to shed light on the dysfunction with unhealthy marriages in an effort to help others avoid similar journeys. To each DND co-author, I say, THANK YOU for choosing to share your powerful experiences within the pages of *Divorced...NOT Devastated*. I am confident that DND will be the impetus to a movement. #DND

Acknowledgements

Giving honor to **God**, who is my true salvation and compass through this thing that we call "life." Being raised Southern Baptist means I had no choice but to go to church as a young child... But I'm so thankful that, somewhere along the journey, God got down deep into my soul and became my foundation and guiding light. I'm thankful for His agape covering, especially as I navigated the waters of my divorce. I am also thankful that he dropped DND on my spirit in 2017 and am thankful for those that he brought to the project to fully round out its literary destiny.

To my village:

- **Erica and Jonathan Green**: You are definitely more than my sister and brother-in-love; you both are the engine to this DND train! You two have morphed into that powerhouse couple poised to change the world: with Erica leading SHERO Publishing and Jonathan blessing us with all things graphic through Greenlight Creations. Thank you for helping to make my DND dreams come true! We definitely wouldn't be holding THIS book without you.

- **Linda and Euric Perry**: Better known as LP and BP, you two are truly the prototype! Thank you for raising me in a God-fearing home built on love and integrity. Thank you for putting up with me, especially during my marriage and divorce. LP, thank you so much for serving as our

Divorced…NOT Devastated

"DND Mama" and lending your priceless services through SynergyEd Consulting. And thank you for being the BEST grandparents in the world; it brings me joy to see our two jewels excitedly in your presence.

- **Chauncey Sanderlin**: You are the daily wind beneath my wings; the constant "why" for any and everything I do. From watching you sleep to our science experiments, being the maternal part of your life journey has been the biggest blessing in my life. Your genuine love for God and zest for life is a true testament to your rich, steadfast foundation. I pray that you continue to grow into your goodness, and know that I'll be right here by your side!

- **Camryn Green**: You cease to amaze me! Each day reveals a new talent: from artist to illustrator to motivational speaker and beyond. Like your "brother-cuz" I relish in the way you share God's love with the world. You constantly make me proud to be your auntie! The sky is the limit for your talents, and I'm here for each and every "In Living Color" moment!

-**Michelle Harris-Jefferson**: To my first accountability partner, thank you for being there for me, even when I didn't know! Until you, I never had someone say "Girl, I don't know what's going on, but I lay prostrate for you today." TRUE friends that take the time out of their busy lives to PRAY for you are priceless! Thanks for being the example and motivating me to share my truth. I love you, AP!

-**Clarissa Johnson**: Words can't express how much your friendship means to me! When others didn't, you navigated the waters and remained a friend to both me and my ex. You also continue to be an AMAZING godmother to prince Chauncey. I look forward to many more years in your presence.

- **Secrick Gibson**: Thank you for your support throughout my divorce. Your daily check-ins, to encourage or tell me about your family's recent vacations, helped give me hope for the future. You may not know it, but those weekly meals actually helped stretch my food budget. I'm eternally grateful for your kindness.

- **Courey Lassiter**: You are the newest piece to my life's puzzle. Though we've known each other practically our entire lives, I am thankful that God brought you back into my life as the brilliant, hard-working, dedicated man that you are today. Thank you for being the supportive impetus behind my new hustle and drive; thank you for always encouraging me to tell my truth. You are the epitome of Fantasia's, "When I Met You."

> "It takes courage....
> to endure the sharp pains of
> self-discovery rather than
> choose to take the dull pain of
> unconsciousness that would last
> the rest of our lives."
>
> —Marianne Williamson

Foreword

Coincidentally, on the day that I penned this piece, my pastor preached a sermon entitled, "The Ten Commandments of Holy Dating." Despite the fact that I have been married forty-one years and have grown closer and more in sync with my husband with each passing year, I found myself feverishly taking notes. My pastor spoke from a biblical perspective but made his message clear and relevant as he drew from personal experience and current research. He created analogies that were both engaging and thought-provoking. His points made sense and could serve to support single members of our congregation to set standards as they navigate through the modern-day complexities of dating. I found myself, using this checklist, to reflect back to my dating experience, all those many years ago. I was intrigued to see how my personal set of guidelines matched up to those detailed in "The Ten Commandments of Holy Dating." I was interested in exploring how shifts in societal norms and expectations had increased the challenges of dating and marriage.

Three months ago, the sermon would not have stimulated such an interest in me, but I had been pulled into a new experience. I had been blessed to be connected to eleven extraordinary women: the women of the "Divorced...NOT Devastated" book project! The visionary behind the project, Kimberly Perry-Sanderlin had been "called" to create this compilation. God's voice was clear, so she prayed. She prayed that God would appoint the right women to this project. God did just that! The eleven women who committed to share their experiences; all were driven by their own unique needs. These phenomenal women came with different stories, yet when they came together, they discovered commonalities that were astounding!

Over the months, I have witnessed these ladies develop trust, respect, and support for each other. They have become a true sisterhood. They have challenged and supported each other; asking the poignant and necessary questions that have evoked new self-discoveries and promoted growth. As a result, they have committed to being transparent in telling their stories so that their truths can connect them with others who are struggling through dating, marriage, and divorce issues. For the DND ladies, it has not been easy to discard masks or to reveal that which they have fought so hard to forget and forgive. However, these ladies, in their newfound strength, have determined that this book is part of their journey; it is part of their healing. In this celebratory stage of their journey, they accept their responsibility to serve others; to give back to other women who are like they were. It is the goal of the DND ladies to empower and to give hope.

Now, as you begin to read, prepare yourself for stories that will cause you to experience a rollercoaster of emotions. One thing that you can count on is that – this book will make a difference.

Linda Simons Perry, Certified Life Coach

Author Kimberly Perry Sanderlin

Kimberly Perry Sanderlin

Over the past 6 years, Kimberly found her professional passions in the areas of teacher mentorship, flipped/blended learning, and curriculum development. With the support of her retired educator parents, Kimberly became CEO/Co-Founder of SynergyEd Consulting Group. Her vision is to create and implement quality educator training worldwide through 21st century tools.

Kimberly is one who does not shy from pursuing all of her passions. She is a National Board Certified Teacher (2013), a NC Kenan Fellow (2013-14), and Fulbright-Hays Group Project Abroad to China Participant (2015). Kimberly is currently 1 of 25 educators appointed to Governor Roy Cooper's Teacher Advisory Committee (2017-19). Kimberly is also a budding photographer; providing all photography for Sisters Lifting Sisters Nonprofit and many Shero Publishing projects.

Although Kimberly is proud of being one of the featured authors in *Unleash Your Shero* (2017), she is immensely proud of being obedient to God and fulfilling the *Divorced... NOT Devastated* book vision. She is excited to continue the DND Mission to empower and encourage separated and divorced women and men to determine and walk victoriously into their ordained futures. The DND Team is currently working on *Divorced... NOT Devastated- The Male Perspective* and *Divorced...*

NOT Devastated Volume II. The team also plans to make a broader impact through its first DND Conference (Fall 2018). Kimberly is also currently working on publishing her *Rapid Root Challenge* educational program and completing her memoir, *God's YESS Through My Mess* (both Spring 2019 releases). Kimberly continues to assist other men and women in sharing their voices through writing; excited to provide book coaching to future Shero Publishing clients.

When Kimberly is not wearing her educator or business hats, she enjoys quality time with family, especially her soon-to-be 6-year-old prince, Chauncey, and her 13-year-old niece, Camryn.

Divorced...NOT Devastated

Sleeping With The Enemy

"I was visiting an old friend... she left her husband... He was a horrible man. He used to **beat** her... At first he was charming, tender. But it all changed... He said if she left him he would punish her, and he meant it..."

- Couldn't she call the police?

Well, she did. She called them, and a lawyer too...

- Well, how did she leave?

She risked everything. Escaped. Started a new life.

- Brave girl.

She thinks she's a coward.

- A coward? Not a girl like that. How long did you stay with him?

Too long. Three years, seven months, six days.

~ Sleeping With the Enemy, 20th Century Fox (1991)

Divorced...NOT Devastated

Anybody who knows me knows that I have a song or movie clip for almost any situation. For me, both can be very therapeutic; at times, as if the precise song or clip is being sent serendipitously from heaven to me as a necessary sign to get my soul or actions in check. I found this to be the case in February 2015 when I flipped through the TV and found one of my favorite movies, *Sleeping With The Enemy*, just starting. As a lover of anything Julia Roberts, this film was always one of my favorite performances by her. Even though I was a mere 8 years old when it debuted, I remember never missing the opportunity to watch it. Always one for a good thriller, my young exposure to the film was purely out of respect for her triumphant ability to escape and SURVIVE. I always get tense when her seemingly charming husband struck her for the first time and she, consequently, attempted to clean up the broken flower vase and mask her scars afterwards. I am on the edge of my seat each time the storm comes at sea and she is thought to have drowned. Then I'm rooting her on when I find that it was a strategically orchestrated escape; one that she'd planned, step-by-step, months prior to her departure. From facing her biggest fear and learning how to swim, to getting her get-away bag ready and stashed and making sure that her elderly mother was safe... she'd played her role until the perfect moment of escape.

The scene referenced above is actually the iconic scene where she's on the bus traveling in disguise to her new town and begins talking to another passenger. She's finally sharing her truth with a stranger that has kindly offered her an apple and harmless discourse. Though I had seen this movie a thousand times before, I found myself crying as I watched her share her experience in third-person; attempting to detach from her own trauma. I cried even more when I calculated how long I'd actually been in my relationship at that time: 7 years, 2 months, and 5 days. Yep: too long!

The sheer shock of the parallels to my own situation had me momentarily emotionally overwhelmed. Once I caught my breath, I began to go into my usual introspective, sociological approach. I got out my notebook and, thanks to my DVR, I rewound the movie to the beginning to see what other parallels I missed. I was shocked!

Divorced...NOT Devastated

1) **Laura Parallels**: From Laura's initial interactions with her husband, you get the sense that she was once a strong woman, full of life... now reduced to a shell as a result of the abuse. Any of my lifelong friends would describe me as very outspoken but one who loved and fully engaged in every moment of life. That was no longer the woman that I saw when I looked in the mirror. The years of emotional isolation from my husband had left me self-conscious. The inebriated, late-night arrivals home- not sure whether it would be a quiet night or one where he'd verbally abuse me or drag our 3 year-old out of bed to lecture him about not choosing a wife like his mother- had left me bitter and jaded. Like Laura, I was able to put on a smile and do "life" outside my house, but was fully uncomfortable as soon as I entered what should have been my sanctuary. That was because I didn't know which husband would show up each evening. Because of this, I had gotten into a cycle of daily highs-and-lows: happy at work (I've ALWAYS loved my career as an educator!), then miserable as I drove home; anticipating the awkward silence or arguments that would greet me at the door.

Divorced...NOT Devastated

Like Laura with her elderly mother, I now had responsibilities outside myself: my 3-year-old prince. This was the hardest thing to acknowledge: the affect that our dysfunction was having on our young son. He had recently been diagnosed with Hyperacusis, a disorder characterized by intolerance of normal environmental sounds (such as vacuums and automatic flushing toilets in public facilities). This disorder had begun to wreak havoc on our young son; causing him to cover his ears and cry when confronted with specific auditory frequencies. My heart dropped and I lost it again when I finally made the connection that WE had contributed to our son's neurological scars. Our late-night screaming could be the environmental factor that now caused Pre-K teachers to wonder why our son took so long in the restroom... too scared to hear the toilet flush or use the automatic hand dryer... because the high decibels subconsciously reminded him of his mommy and daddy screaming on the other side of the house. Although I would do anything to make sure my son was safe- from keeping him with me as much as possible after finding out his father would drink and drive, even with our young child in the car, to starving myself to make sure he ate- our union still had major effects on our offspring.

Divorced...NOT Devastated

Finally, like Laura, the marriage had taken a major emotional and physical toll on me. Although physical abuse was not an issue- at least not for me (you'll have to read *Unleash Your Shero* to fill in those puzzle pieces), emotional and financial abuse were constant. On the emotional front, I mainly was in a constant state of FEAR and EMBARRASSMENT. Fear as to what my husband would do in public. For example, during our early years together, we'd begun coaching together and were very successful; with 3 district championships under our belt for two different sports by our second year. During most of our coaching career, he was coaching under my name and credentials; either because he wasn't a licensed teacher or because the available positions were at my school. However, in our last two years together, my husband had become increasingly combative with other coaches, and at times, had less-than-professional interactions with parents and players. I always found myself running interference, or covering up his behavior. His inappropriate behavior came to a head in 2016 when he initiated a *back-and-forward* with an opposing coach. I was employed by a strong, responsive principal, who quickly called my ex into her office the next day and explained what would *not* be tolerated and the expectations for professionalism. Of course, he put on the charm and apologized

Divorced…NOT Devastated

(something he never did within our relationship). Thankfully, they addressed his inappropriate behavior, but it was still a scar on my reputation, since I was the coach-of-record. Even in a large district, educators talk and news travels fast… I could not afford for him to continue to damage the career that I loved.

Because many of our friends were colleagues, and because his alcoholism was becoming evident in social settings, I began to ignore invites to activities as a safeguard, or rather, a band-aid against the truth. Every now and then, he'd be in a peak and re-assure me that he was sober again… just to show up at the event intoxicated and causing me to cringe in anticipation of his erratic behavior. He had a collection of 1-month sober coins to prove the cycle from alcoholic, to recovering to "fuck it! I don't need AA!" and back again.

Whether he was drunk and getting loud at a friend's house party, or passive-aggressively commenting negatively about my coaching moves in front of our teams or parents, the emotional abuse left me extremely embarrassed. Though I pride myself in living in integrity, I now had a soul-tie and marriage vows with someone who'd gone from "honest Abe" to the biggest liar you could find. His dishonesty started off being isolated to simply covering up his alcoholism... but once, he got good at that, he began lying about everything. (He once told our marriage counselor that "he'd lie about the color of the sky.") Because the truth was so important to me, I began to loathe his presence and expressed it through my body language and actions. His deceitful nature collided head-on with my Type-A personality. The more he lied about being at AA meetings or lied about the female on the other end of his phone, the more I built up a wall between us. Instead of going to God like I'd been trained to do in the face of adversity, I'd begun to "go low" and toe-to-toe with my monster. We became toxic people; spewing our hate and hurt in and outside of our home. We were short with our sweet prince and anybody else around us.

My family felt the brunt of our dysfunction. Because my ex had limited actions with his own family, all holidays and major experiences were with my parents and my sister's family. We all attended the same amazing church. At the beginning of our marriage, it was nothing to see our family almost take up an entire row- with my ex happily present and praising the Lord. He actually was baptized a few years after our wedding; a happy day for us all. But when his drinking increased and began to affect every aspect of his life, he stopped attending church. Even with funds increasingly tight, church was my solace and escape. I'd pack up my son and usually spend the night at either my sister's or parent's home, so my son and I could attend church together. Although I didn't notice it at the time, my parents later reminded me that they would have to almost force me to go back home Sunday evenings; their first sign that my marriage was falling apart... When they'd ask what was going on, I would snap, yelling "Nothing! Just leave me alone!" These were the individuals who were quietly financially supporting my family when our household income was affected by my husband's frequent under-employment or unwillingness to adequately contribute to family bills.

Although emotional abuse is enough, it was the financial abuse that had the largest effect on our household and my health. As I continued to rise in my career, my husband continued to digress. As a lateral entry educator, he found it difficult to secure licensure and stay employed. Although varied excuses were given, he always was one of the first to get transferred when surplus moves were made. Though he never talked to me about the situations, it's hard to think alcoholism didn't play a part in at least one of his moves... especially after I found two cold 24-

Divorced...NOT Devastated

ounce beers in his open car at lunch time, as I was attempting to retrieve needed paperwork from the vehicle. When I confronted him, he put the focus on why I hadn't waited until he got home to get the paperwork, instead of addressing why he had the equivalent of 4 beers waiting for him when he got off work... and since they were cold, explaining when he'd purchased them. I reminded my ex that I needed the paperwork to get a ticket dropped that I had acquired the day I drove his car to work and got stopped for *his* expired tags.

The more employment changes that he had, the more he seemed to drink and emotionally shield himself from me. His new routine was coming home late, with his eyes glazed over. To avoid me, he'd go immediately to the sofa and begin watching Netflix, but was usually asleep within an hour. He'd wake in the morning, usually silent or mustering a cold "good morning," and start the same cycle over again. Though he was supposed to be actively working on his classes for his licensure, his focus was usually on coaching (which was not a necessity but his love) or Netflix. Then he'd begin working on licensure assignments an hour or so before they were due. Frequently, he would attempt to get me to assist with his last-minute assignments, on top of my own increasing responsibilities. Because I knew he'd wasted time that could have been dedicated to his licensure pursuits, I was vocal about his wasted time, which angered him and usually induced a late-night argument. It was purely exhausting!

When he ran out of time for his licensure, he was reduced from a Teacher back to a Teacher Assistant. This reduction was an immediate financial shock; decreasing our household income by $8,000! Being on a two-teacher budget was already tight enough... having our household income decreased by $800 per month was frightening! Though I didn't know how bad it was until I saw old FB timeline photos, or my hair stylist pointed it out, I began to lose weight that I didn't have to lose and began to experience stress bald patches on my scalp. Although I always had a few hustles going- from my educational consulting to my photography - he didn't jump to make up the difference. I had to urge him to get a part-time job and prepare his resume to apply for positions. He never secured a part-time job, with his excuse being that he was now required to take additional classes to re-establish his ability to teach. He outright told me that he felt he "shouldn't have to work on his degree and have a part-time job." So I did the only thing I could do: I continued to trim the fat where possible. I stopped getting my hair done, even though he still got professional haircuts. I cut off the cable and I began using my summer funds for the shortage.

When we'd get close to having our heads afloat, my checking account would mysteriously be over-drafted and would not match my meticulous budget checklist, or my credit card would be maxed out when I hadn't used it in over a year! Initially, I asked my ex if he knew what was going on, and he'd always shout "No! Why are you accusing me?!" Finally, when the statement showed a withdrawal that I couldn't have made due to location and time, he confessed to taking the cards and withdrawing money from my personal account and credit card as desired for his personal needs. This, coupled with the fact that he saw fit to continue volunteer coaching at the YMCA instead of securing a part-time job were the last nails in the coffin of our marriage.

At the end of the film, I looked at my +/- chart, which was saturated with the negatives within our marriage, and I realized, like Laura, that it was time for my escape plan! The film gave me supernatural clarity; the film had served as my metaphorical on/off switch... I wiped away my tears, and with them, my excuses and complacency. The date was October 28, 2015.

The first thing I did was document the actions that had been taken to salvage our marriage. First, I had supported his participation in AA when he initiated it; even attending the first AA meeting with him as support, and attending Al-Anon family meetings individually. I was supportive throughout his rollercoaster of being an alcoholic one day and "in control" the next. I found out later that he went through a cycle of starting and stopping AA, which explained the numerous 1 and 2-month Sobriety coins that I found later on in the house. Next, we both sought individual counseling to deal with our own issues. Of course, this therapy was largely one-sided, with me continuing after he quit. Through my own individual counseling and our marriage counseling, I had received clarity- it takes two to tango. In the sessions, my ex never acknowledged his drinking, and when the counselor pointed out his "passive-aggressive behavior," he declared that he was being "ganged up on" by the counselor and me, and he stopped going to sessions. I found out later that the counselor was also his personal counselor and had led several sessions

Divorced...NOT Devastated

individually with him before I was "invited" into what I assumed was separate marriage counseling.

Next, I implemented a solo budget, realizing that my largest fear and what probably kept me trapped longer than I needed to be in our failing marriage, was not being able to sustain myself and my child on one income. Thankfully, I had already been adjusting to his dwindling contributions to the household. I was shocked when I realized that my solo budget, coupled with some new professional projects, only left a $300 shortage; proving that he had become financial deadweight in our household! This motivated me to move on the next step: declaring a need to separate.

About 2 weeks later, when my son was strategically with my sister for the weekend, I calmly asked my ex to talk with me. I declared that it was clear that we both had been unhappy for quite some time, and that I thought we should separate. I told him that he could have the house, (even though I knew I'd probably lose it due to his financial state. He totally ignored his personal bills and currently was not in a situation to pay a mortgage), and I'd look for another place. He quickly declared that he didn't want the house and I was overreacting. I assured him that I was

Divorced...NOT Devastated

not overreacting and that I wouldn't change my mind. I told him since he didn't want the house, I'd be glad to help him locate alternate housing. I pulled out a document that I had researched and prepared of 30+ rental options that were under $300 and close enough that he could see his son daily if he'd like. I think he was so shocked by my calmness, preparedness, and persistence that he agreed to begin looking for alternate housing. Because I didn't trust that he'd follow through without me present, we silently rode together in the car to each of the rentals that he agreed to see. I even made it clear that I'd pay his first and last month rent, even though I'd have to borrow money to make it happen... Although he did sabotage some opportunities by purposefully not showing up to scheduled viewings (with people texting me because his phone was off at the time), we did end up with 2-3 viable options.

The final thing that I did in preparation to escape was research and prepare a Separation Agreement. Because I barely had money to pay bills, I tweaked a template I found online. The main things I wanted outlined in the separation agreement were:

- Ensuring I had custody of my son until his father FULLY dealt with his alcoholism

Divorced...NOT Devastated

- Ensuring I maintained full ownership of my second car and my house (which had been purchased prior to marriage and was solely in my name). I gave him my first car, even though my dad had purchased it for me as a high school graduation gift. Other than that, I didn't care what happened with anything, and felt that we could deal with everything else at a later time.

Thankfully, one of my sister's close friends was a lawyer. She reviewed The Separation Agreement and said it looked good and that she'd be praying he would sign it. None of us thought that he would, but I prayed earnestly for a miracle. I started claiming this as our last Christmas together. I didn't want my last gesture within our marriage to be a negative one. I also wanted to soften his heart before presenting the document. Even though I could've used the money on something else, I knew Kobe Bryant and the Lakers were playing in Charlotte. The tickets were ridiculous, but I dropped $250 on a mid-grade ticket for my ex to attend the game. I presented the ticket to him on Christmas and he was over-the-moon excited. I guess he didn't expect it either, because he hadn't reciprocated. This had become the norm; if we'd had an argument within weeks of any holiday or birthday, he didn't get a gift for me, even

Divorced...NOT Devastated

though I always had one for him! With him excited about his upcoming game, I presented him with the separation papers on the morning of December 28, 2015. I don't know if he thought I'd changed my mind, but he initially refused to sign. Although I tried to hold back my emotions, I remember crying and shouting that we had to separate. Finally I honestly said that our marriage was killing me (which it was if you count the major weight loss, hair loss, and frequent sickness) and damaging our son. I emphasized the fact that we could attempt to salvage our marriage, but that I could not go into the new year without separating. I honestly expressed that I hoped we could work at salvaging our marriage, but that we both knew we needed time apart. He passive-aggressively read the document aloud in front of me and agreed to get it notarized. He suggested that we "get it done tomorrow" because it was the day of the game, but I reminded him that there was plenty of time to get it done and still make the game. He packed up the majority of his belongings in the one suitcase that he had and multiple heavy-duty trash bags. Internally giddy, I helped him pack as much as he would allow.

Divorced...NOT Devastated

We drove to the nearest FedEx, where I had checked a day before to make sure they had a notary public on duty. It was a super-quick process. He followed me to my car and held my door open to profess that he was "committed to fighting for his family." I said "okay" and after showing him how to use his GPS to get to Charlotte, we went our separate ways.

The day was similar to the majority of our marriage: for him pleasure, and for me WORK! I was on the phone before I pulled out of the FedEx parking lot: calling my family and exciting declaring "Praise God! He signed!" I texted the family friend and thanked her and told her he'd signed. She was shocked as well, but confessed to praying for a miracle, too. Within a few hours, the locks were changed and his remaining items in the house were boxed up. I did NOT plan on making our Separation Agreement null and void; knowing that we had to live separately for it to remain solid. I knew he had options and could at least find a place to stay for the night. I even put a mutual family friend on alert, to make sure he'd have a place to stay for the first night.

I only had a few hours to celebrate; there definitely was no time to exhale… He arrived back home around 1:30am in the morning and attempted to put his key in the lock. He knocked lightly but I was at the

Divorced...NOT Devastated

door to remind him that we could not live together, according to our agreement. I could tell he had been drinking. (Sidenote: It always amazed me that he made it home safely as much as he did! Though he couldn't keep hubcaps on the car and would come home with mysterious dents and fender-benders, I was thankful because it could have been much worse!) I reminded him that he had options and that I was willing to assist. He said "I don't need your help!" and left. He came by drunk about two days later, banging on my bedroom window and begging me to "let him in" claiming it was "cold" and that he'd been "sleeping in his car." I told him that he was going to wake up our son, so he eventually left. About a week later, he called begging to come back because he had been kicked out of his rental apartment. When I asked why, he could never give a straight answer. I never asked where he was staying, but whenever possible, he made sure to tell our 3-year old that he was "homeless". This became one of the first subjects addressed when my son started counseling and one of his father's first attempts to victimize himself and paint me as the villain ("If daddy is homeless, why won't mommy let him come back home?").

Divorced...NOT Devastated

Still not able to exhale, I began my RECOVERY. About a week before our separation, I passed a local church and read "Divorce Care" on their marquee. I declared to myself that, if God made the separation happen, I was going to devote myself to THAT recovery program. I was legally separated on December 28, 2015 and started the 10-week program on January 5, 2016. It was exactly what both my son and I needed. We turned every Tuesday night into our mommy-son special night; with us stopping at Chick-Fil-A for food and play before each session. Divorce Care provided FREE childcare, which allowed me to focus on the sessions without having to worry about another financial burden. Though each session had practical topics, such as FINANCES or SEXUALITY AFTER DIVORCE, each was connected to several scriptures. We also formed small groups for discussion. I remember starting the sessions in such a cloudy place. My turning point was the day that I was introduced to Jeremiah 3:8: *I gave faithless Israel her certificate of divorce and sent her away because of all her adulteries...* Again, it was like a switch was turned on in me! I was reminded that, though God dislikes divorce, He knows when it is necessary. Although I had been devoted to the program, it was that moment that made me re-examine the state of my devotion to God. I soon realized that my relationship with God needed to be priority. I

Divorced...NOT Devastated

began praying consistently again, both privately and by establishing a strong prayer routine with my son. We listened to nothing but gospel, which caused a spiritual shift for us both; with my son becoming calmer both at school and home. After Divorce Care ended, I started Divorce Recovery, another faith-based program that ran 8 weeks. I also found my son a counselor and started bi-monthly counseling for him. By the end of the 4 months of divorce counseling, I truly was a new person and my son was on the way to developing coping skills for his new life.

I wish I could say the drama between me and my ex-husband ended with our separation. For months, he would berate me with dozens of text messages; usually sent during his witching hours (10pm-1am). After a night when he sent me 40+ unanswered texts- telling me what secrets he was going to divulge to everyone I knew- I finally learned how to block my phone during my sleeping hours; with the only folks being able to get through being my family.

Early on when the hurt was raw, and he was lying and threatening me- everything from, "Your whole family is going to hell!" to "I'll sue you for what you did to me (see *Unleash*)!"- I would go back and forth, toe-to-toe with him. But about 4 weeks into my Divorce Recovery classes, they

Divorced...NOT Devastated

addressed the "Types & Stages of Anger" and I was able to realize that my attempts were futile. Although he sends similar messages from time-to-time, such as a rant sent recently when he began assuming I was dating, I ignore all that do not deal with our son. Although, we are still at different stages in our recovery, I do pray that he will one day mend his now non-existent relationship with our son.

Like Laura's husband, my ex was very charming and the daily lies were convincing to those outside our tumultuous marriage. I moved to another school within the district after a sexual incident with him and a former colleague, but our drama began to seep into my new sanctuary. I was now an 8th grade teacher team leader under great administrators and working alongside great colleagues. In retrospect, the mistake was my own because, in financial distress, we continued to team coach at my new school, which kept my ex connected with me professionally; and at a time when his alcoholism was peaking. One day my accountability partner (AP) and good friend and colleague called me at home and told me that one of the substitute teachers on the 6th grade hall that day had been looking for me. Long-story-short, she was looking for me so that she could talk to me about "putting my husband out." (My ex corroborated

Divorced...NOT Devastated

the event some months later.) Though the substitute teacher's attempt was wrong on so many levels, I was thankful that (1) my AP blocked the interaction because I wasn't stable enough to deal with the substitute teacher professionally and (2) it taught me the type of dishonest interactions that my ex was having with others as it related to our former marriage. I alerted my administrators that I needed a change and found an awesome job in Durham Public Schools. I had just enough money to relocate closer to family in Wake County. The new job, my son's new school, and being close to family has been just what my son and I both needed as we continue along our journey to recovery. Instead of coming home anxious and fearful for what awaits, I now come home excited to share the day with my son and other members of our village. Just the other day my son snuggled with me and said "Mommy, I'm glad we moved to Raleigh! I love my life!" It made EVERYTHING over the last 2 years worthwhile...

Lessons Learned

1) **Seek God first in any relationship**: As I transparently became an active participant in my recovery, I learned a LOT about myself. I learned that I had a lot of shit that was not reconciled about self before jumping into my marriage. For example, I had fractured relationships with my parents that indirectly played a role within my marriage. Having clarity and good counseling allowed me the structure to evaluate my issues and the strength to ask for forgiveness. It also taught me that I was in a relationship that God did not ordain, which makes it almost impossible to expect success.

2) **Forgive yourself:** This is an imperative step. I entered "Divorce Care" ashamed that I was now a statistic. The cloud was not lifted in my life until I genuinely forgave myself.

3) **Forgive your ex-spouse:** As hard as this may be, it has to be done before you can begin to fully heal and get closure in your failed marriage. It also allows you to begin to see them through a more objective lens, which allows you to extend them grace more freely. This will prove to be

a necessity, especially if your ex struggles with passive-aggressive or more volatile tendencies.

4) **What about the kids?!:** Be aware that the divorce does not just affect you and your spouse, especially if kids are involved. You have to prioritize their emotions and need for recovery measures. Also do not bad-mouth the other parent. As hard as it may be to hold in your subjectivity, allow your child to formulate their own opinion about their other parent through experience ONLY.

5) **Make a plan:** Like Laura and me, you must be as PREPARED as possible going into a separation or divorce. You know your ex better than most, so use what you know about them to get the best outcome. I had to be honest and realize that I had enabled my ex for years; even down to preparing his resume and applying for jobs for him. As a result, I stifled his independence, and had to assist him more in transitioning to life outside our marriage. It is also imperative to develop a budget and recovery plan.

I pray that my experiences are a blessing to you along your own journey.

Author Takiya Lewis

Takiya Lewis

Takiya Lewis is an attorney practicing in Eastern North Carolina, where she was born and raised. She earned a B.A. in English from North Carolina Agricultural and Technical State University. After completing her undergraduate degree, she attended North Carolina Central University School of Law, where she graduated with her Juris Doctorate in 2010.

After graduating from law school, she returned to Eastern North Carolina to practice law; dedicated to providing legal services to the residents of the area. In 2012, she opened her own law practice, where she practices criminal and civil law.

She is a member of the North Carolina State Bar, the North Carolina State Bar Association and Alpha Kappa Alpha Sorority, Incorporated. In her spare time, she likes to read, write and travel.

While she wears many hats, her favorite is the one she wears as a parent. She is a mother of one child, a rambunctious little boy named Peyton.

Disappearing Acts

I never thought I would get divorced. I thought I would get married. I thought I would have children. I thought that I would have a career. I never thought of those things not happening the way I saw them in my head. My journey with my ex-husband started when I was 22 years old. It's funny when you're young; you think you have life and the world all figured out. It never, ever occurs to you that you have no idea what life has in store for you.

When I met my ex-husband, I thought that I had begun the part of my journey that would lead me to marriage and children. Since I had been accepted into law school, I figured my career path was set- I just needed to figure out my personal life. I started dating my ex about a month before law school started. I felt like I was on cloud nine. In my mind, I had finally found a person with whom to have a real relationship. Looking back now, I see there were signs that maybe things weren't as wonderful as I wanted them to be. After we had been dating for several months, I told him that I loved him. His response to me was, "Are you sure?". Insert a blank stare here. While that hurt me, it wasn't enough for me to throw in the towel. I mean, everyone moves at their own pace right?!

Divorced...NOT Devastated

Of course, hindsight is 20/20 and that one moment sums up the lack of commitment that I feel was the most serious issue we faced in our relationship. When I say lack of commitment, I mean that I wanted the security of knowing that we were going to be together, no matter what. That was definitely not the case. We broke up several times during the course of our dating relationship. In fact, I felt like we were always breaking up and getting back together. A repetitive pattern. It seemed that every time things were getting serious between us, we would break up. Every time I wanted more, he pushed me away. However, love is blind and there was not a person walking this Earth that could have told me, I was not in love with him.

The last time we broke up, we broke up for about 6 months. At that point, I figured we had reached the point of no return. I was tired of breaking up and getting back together so I figured he was too. Apparently, we were tired, but not tired enough. He contacted me one day and asked me to meet him, so I did. He told me what most girls dream of hearing from the man with whom they're in love. He told me that he loved me and wanted to marry me and that I was the one for him. At that point, I was overjoyed—a little skeptical—but overjoyed, nonetheless. The love that I had for him caused me to overlook everything that had gone wrong in our relationship in the past. I put my blinders on and looked only toward the future. I mean, why would he tell me he wanted to marry me and not mean it?!

Divorced...NOT Devastated

We got married shortly before I graduated law school and had to start studying for the bar exam. One thing that I always craved from him was consistency. I wanted him to be there, every day. I wanted him to love me and want me the way that I loved and wanted him. I wanted stability. And that included emotional and financial stability. We were both at transitional stages in our lives and at that point, he did not have a full-time job that could support us. After taking the bar, the job that I got was back home. Since that was the only job prospect either of us had, it seemed like a no brainer. Prior to me getting hired, we had discussed the possibility of moving back to our small town if he was unable to find a job. I thought we were both on the same page. But again, I was wrong about what pages we were actually on...

He decided that he didn't want to move back home. He didn't want to leave the city we were in and go back to our small town. I couldn't deny that I had those same feelings, but someone had to be the grown-up and be realistic about our situation. Still, my ex insisted that he wasn't going to move back home. He was going to continue to work at his dead-end job and stay with friends while I moved home. That absolutely hurt me. We were supposed to be a team, but he left me to fend for myself and be alone; all because small town life was not what he wanted. The hurt and anger that I felt was real. Looking back, I can see that it was so much more than him deciding not to move with me. It was just another episode of: *when the going got tough, my ex got going.*

Divorced...NOT Devastated

After moving back home, our marriage was up and down. He received a job offer that didn't have a real job description. At first, he was going to be in one state, then that changed. He didn't know how long the job was going to last or if it was permanent. Then instead of being stationary, he was going to be moving around. Considering the fact that our relationship was so inconsistent, I was not confident enough or secure enough in our relationship to deal with the lack of specifics about his job. I don't think I was completely unreasonable. When he believed that the job was going to be in one place, I sucked it up and told him I would move with him. I agreed even though I had just passed the bar and would have to take another bar exam to work in a different state. But when it once again became uncertain that he would be positioned in one location, I got scared. I didn't have faith that if anything happened and things became difficult that he would put me and our marriage first. I asked him not to go. He told me he was going anyway. That truly marked the beginning of the end of our marriage.

I was so hurt, so scared and so angry. How could he leave like that? We had just gotten married. We were still technically newlyweds. At this point, he had already shown me twice, that he was going to put his wants and interests before our marriage. How could I not feel like he was going to do the same thing he always did when things got serious? We tried to make it work while he was gone, but I was so angry and so hurt. I needed acknowledgement from him. I just wanted him to say that he understood where I was coming from and why I felt the way I did. For better or worse, that wasn't something that was going to happen.

Divorced...NOT Devastated

We ended up separating a little while after he left. I remember telling him that we were married, and he couldn't just break up with me. His response was he could if he wanted to. Even though we had technically separated, I still wore my ring because in my heart, I wasn't ready to be separated. The day I took my ring off, he had come back into town and we were sitting in the car talking. He told me that I was playing myself for wanting to be with him and he was playing himself for wanting to be with me. I was heartbroken. I had never felt more lost or lonely. I was devastated. But I didn't want to allow myself to feel that depth of emotion. I didn't want to hurt the way I was hurting. I wanted to ignore the pain. Pretend that I was okay. Even though my marriage was ending, and my world as I knew it was over, I wanted to pretend that I was fine. So I pretended. I let anger be the main emotion that I felt so that I could pretend that my love for him was gone. I wanted to hate him, so I did. That was my way of feeling better and hiding from my emotions. That masquerade turned out to be one of the worse things I could have ever done.

Several months after we separated, I met someone. He was completely different than my ex. He wanted to talk to me and be with me all the time. He seemed like he genuinely cared for me. However, his wanting to spend time with me and talk to me turned into obsession. It went from him calling me because he wanted to talk, to him calling me several times a day and me having to talk to him so he could be assured I wasn't cheating. Being with someone who had so many insecurities and control issues was new to me. Because it was new, I didn't recognize it

Divorced...NOT Devastated

for what it really was. I didn't realize how bad it was until I got pregnant and moved to Georgia to be with him. I was there for 3 months and can only remember going to one place by myself. I literally could not use the bathroom for longer than two minutes before he would come bursting in. I left a couple of times, but because I was pregnant, I went back. It got to the point that we ended up having a physical altercation and I moved back home that same day.

Right after that happened, I spoke to my ex. I confessed that I was pregnant, and he was supportive. At that point, I was divorced, pregnant, jobless, and depressed. I was probably in the worse situation I had ever been in. After I had my son, my ex came to see me. We reconnected and found ourselves spending time together, for a while, following that visit. I realized at that point that I still loved him and wanted to be with him. After everything, getting divorced and having my son, I still had hope that my ex and I could make it work. But like always, as easily as he came back into my life, he left it. That was the recipe for our relationship over the course of the next several years.

It was pretty much like clockwork. Once a year, he would pop back up and we would have a mini-courtship until things were getting too serious. He would come back saying he loved me and wanted to work things out. We would spend time getting to know one another once again. Then, I would stop hearing from him. That is, until the next year rolled around and we went through the same song and dance again. This went on for a few years until the last time. For me, it had to be the last time. I had literally spent years getting my hopes up and my heart broken

Divorced...NOT Devastated

by him. For me to be able to truly get through it, I had to look at myself and question why I would continue to do the same things with him, time and time again. I was doing the same thing expecting a different result, but not wanting to acknowledge the insanity in it all. I finally allowed myself time to do some self-reflection. I went over our relationship to really think about the things that I felt I did right and the things that I felt I did incorrectly. I realized that a part of healing and growing is accepting the mistakes you may have made and trying not to repeat them in the future.

Even when I was apart from my ex, he still had a hold over me and I'm sure he never even knew it. When we weren't together, I was angry and sad. In my mind, we could be together if he would just let us. If only he would stop being so noncommittal and admit that he wanted me, we could live happily ever after. I found myself hoping against hope that he would come back. When reality finally hit me and I realized that he just wasn't the one for me, it opened doors for things that I didn't know were possible. I stopped being angry. I accepted that he was who he was and that he was not going to be able to be who I wanted him to be. I became okay with the fact that we weren't going to be together. I felt like I was never going to find someone to love me. It took me a while to realize that yes, he loved me, but not enough. He didn't love me the way that I needed to be loved. And while I loved him, I obviously wasn't loving him the way he needed to be loved.

Once I began to allow myself to really think about things and do some self-evaluation, I realized that almost everything I did was to keep

Divorced...NOT Devastated

from feeling hurt. Every time I chose to let him back in, I did so because I thought that would finally keep my heart from hurting. I didn't want to accept the fact that we were never going to make it work. Every choice I made was to keep from acknowledging the fact that my marriage had failed, and my heart was broken. I thought that if I kept moving and kept myself numb, I would be able to get over the death of my marriage without having to deal with it emotionally. I thought that time would do all the work without me having to show up. I was wrong. Even though time can heal wounds, it can't heal them if you keep them hidden away. I thought that I was saving myself from the pain, but I ended up causing myself more pain in the long run. I essentially lost who I was and what I wanted and needed because I was hiding from myself. It was not until I felt everything, the good and the bad, that I started to come back to being me. I became a stronger and better me because I was able to find myself again.

All these things that I went through were a part of my necessary journey. They were a part of my journey that I couldn't understand when they were happening. I learned so many things since my divorce that I think allowed me to change my life and the way I look at love. I know who I am now. I know what love looks like to me and what I need to be happy. I think I was so blinded by what I thought I wanted, I couldn't see what I needed. When I finally allowed myself to see, to feel, I began to see the journey that I was on. I thought I lost myself in my desire to have the ideal relationship. I could not have been more wrong. Everything I went through ended up being a part of my love story with myself, and I wouldn't change that for anything. The things that I learned are so simple, but it took me going through hell and back to learn them. Of the many lessons, here are a few of the most important things that I keep with me.

Allow yourself to feel. It hurts. It hurts a lot. It will probably hurt for a long time. I know I have the propensity to try and shut my emotions off so I don't feel because I don't want to hurt. If you don't feel the hurt, you also won't feel the healing. You won't know the joy that comes from that one day waking up and being fine; being fine with yourself, with your flaws, with your decisions and with your lessons.

Take your time. And time is relative. Just because it took someone two years to get over their heartbreak, it doesn't mean that you have to take the same amount of time. You may need six months or six years. The thing about taking your time is that it is YOUR time.

Don't allow your broken heart to make your decisions. We all want to feel loved; even more so once we've lost someone that we thought we were going to love until our dying days when we both would be old and gray. It's easy to do things that in your head you know are not the right thing, but you submit because your heart wants to feel whole again.

Open yourself up again. Going through a serious breakup can almost feel like a death. The death of your relationship. The death of your dreams. The death of your future. In many ways, it is that. The life that you thought you would have is gone. But it is also like a birth. You are given the chance to start anew. And while it's hard, it's a new beginning that can change your life for the better.

Have fun. When all the dust has settled, and your heart is up for it, enjoy yourself. I don't mean necessarily by going on dates or starting a new relationship. You can have fun by taking the time to do the things you haven't done in a really long time. Read. Shop. Travel. Do the things that make you happy. Life is about being happy. Be happy.

Author Natasha Perry

Divorced...NOT Devastated

Natasha Perry

Natasha's strong values instilled in her by her wonderful parents, Willie and Barbara Perry, played a fundamental role in her achievements, which include a bachelor's degree in computer science, minor in mathematics as well as a graduate degree in management information systems. Natasha has worked in the Information Technology field for fifteen years.

One of her greatest accomplishments is being one of the co-authors of the collaborative book, *Unleash Your Shero*. Through transparency, Natasha shared her personal testimony and is humbled that it has been a blessing to others. She has a strong relationship with God and is always there to provide encouragement to others who need support.

Natasha is passionate in her pursuits to make a positive change in our communities. She is an advocate for the *Now We No* campaign that spreads awareness about the complications caused by the current feminine products on the market. She enjoys being able to tell women about *Cherish* products which offer a healthy alternative and makes it possible that women no longer have to suffer in silence. Natasha is also a proud member of Alpha Kappa Alpha Sorority, Inc. which provides her additional opportunities to serve others. With pride, she declares that she is the proud aunt of three amazing nephews! Natasha shows what can be

Divorced...NOT Devastated

achieved through perseverance, humility, wisdom, and God's everlasting love.

To learn more about Natasha and her businesses visit these sites:

Instagram – www.instagram.com/empower614

Traci Lynn Jewelry - www.tracilynnjewelry.com/natashaperry

Now We No Campaign- http://nowweno.net/#about

Cherish Products- www.cherishyourselfperiod.com

Shalamar - The Second Time Around lyrics

But you can't keep

Running away from love

Cause the first one

Let you down, no, no, no

And though others

Try to satisfy you, baby

With me, true love

Can still be found

Love can still be found

(The second time around) ooh

The second time is

So much better, baby

(The second time around)

And I make it better

Than the first time

From the Pauper to the Prince

I had heard this song a thousand times during my life, but this time it struck me differently. It felt like he was talking directly to me. After my divorce, I told God that I never wanted another relationship. I was perfectly fine with not getting married again. My plan was to just live my life and adopt a child when I turned forty. You are probably wondering what would make me feel so strongly about NEVER wanting to be in another relationship. Well, let me provide a clear picture of the marriage that I left. Initially, my ex-husband treated me well and he would do anything for me. This charade lasted until we were married. The first indication that showed me that my thoughts and feelings didn't really matter was when he proposed. Now, I know you are probably thinking, "How is that possible? He just proposed. That is the most romantic gesture of all." During his proposal he did tell me how much I meant to him and he loved me so much. When he opened that box and presented a ring, I had to keep it together. He had asked me to find a ring that I liked, and he would buy it for me. I had spent a large amount of time looking for the perfect ring. I didn't want the traditional solitaire ring and I let him know that was the only style that I didn't want.

Divorced...NOT Devastated

Guess what, that is exactly what he bought. At first, I wasn't even going to say anything. I know that the ring isn't the important part. It was about the love that we had for each other and the marriage itself. I never once said anything about the fact that he got the exact ring that I didn't want, but I did ask him how he decided to get this one. He told me that he had picked out two and he let one of his classmates decide between the two rings. Then he bought the one his classmate picked. I couldn't even believe what I was hearing. Again, I kept assuring myself that it wasn't about the ring. So, I pushed my feelings aside about the ring. Now, I see it differently. It wasn't about the ring. It was about him doing whatever he wanted at the expense of my feelings.

Nevertheless, we continued with our marriage plans. We went through several sessions of pre-marriage counseling and everything seemed perfect. He never did any of the assignments ahead of time, but always had the perfect answers during the sessions. His act was so good that the pastor said, "We were meant to be together." My first night as a married woman proved that to be untrue. I spent that night alone crying myself to sleep, wondering what I had gotten myself into. If I had been thinking straight, I would have shredded up those marriage papers while he was gone. Hindsight is 20/20. The next day, he came back with his apologies and excuses, but nothing he said took away the pain. That began the cycle of lies and deceit. His constant drinking and excessive smoking didn't help either. Even though I was the main breadwinner, I was kept under his thumb. He would come home drunk and would adamantly tell me that he was just out with his friends and he wasn't cheating. I never

Divorced...NOT Devastated

once asked him if he was cheating. I guess that was his guilty conscious. He was able to go out and act like he was single, while I was to stay at home. Even going to visit my family was a problem for him. His jealousy and insecurities ran deep. I never told anyone about what was happening because the pastor said that whatever happens in your marriage stays between you two. People kept saying that the first 2-5 years are the hardest. So, I thought this was normal. I had never heard of emotional abuse. I figured since he wasn't physically abusing me, this was acceptable. It wasn't until I started talking to other people that I realized that I was in an unhealthy marriage. It got to the point that I couldn't think of one happy moment in our marriage. I prayed all the time for God to repair my marriage and make my husband into the man I needed him to be. The fact of the matter was that this marriage wasn't in God's will. Anything that isn't in His will can't last.

Despite all that I experienced, the decision to separate wasn't easy. I valued the sanctity of marriage and the vows that I had said before God. I went to two separate therapists and both said that I was in an unhealthy marriage. They recommended that I start a trial separation. After a few months of being separated, the answer was very clear. The peace that I had when I wasn't around my husband spoke for itself. So, I decided to file for divorce. He tried to talk me into coming back. What he failed to realize was that I knew that he was seeing someone else. I had seen them together several times. His constant calls and emails telling me that I was the best thing that had ever happened to him, fell on deaf ears. His actions just confirmed that I was making the right decision. This man

Divorced...NOT Devastated

didn't care about me. What we had was not love. When I finally received the divorce papers, I felt like a child on Christmas. I almost threw a Divorce Party, but my best friend, Denee talked me out it. So, it was the emotional abuse and constant lies that I endured during my marriage that caused me to never want another relationship. Anyone that knows God, knows that he can make beauty from your brokenness. Just because I gave up on love, didn't mean God gave up. He provided love that I never thought I would ever experience.

However, the journey to the healthy relationship had a few bumps in the road. At the beginning of 2015, I decided that I would try online dating; it proved to be a complete disaster! What I realized from my experience with online dating, is that most of the guys on those sites didn't seem to be looking for a serious relationship. Most seemed to just be looking for a hook-up. The initial message that I would get from them would be something like this, "Hello beautiful, do you want to come over?". In my mind, I'm thinking, "I don't know you and you don't know me, why would I want to come over? I could be a serial killer or vice versa. People are just inviting perfect strangers into their homes these days." This happened repeatedly. There was one guy who seemed to be different than the rest. I decided to give him a chance and go out on a date with him. After our first date, I totally understood why he was still single. He had a very strong male chauvinistic personality and a lot of his conversation just didn't make sense. I would talk to guys from work about the things he said, and they even thought this guy was unstable. I really wanted to like him. He was very attractive, but I just couldn't get past his personality. So, needless to say, I didn't talk to him long. I closed my online dating account after about a month. It was a waste of time for me.

Then I met what seemed to be a nice guy at the car dealership. He also was divorced and was a Christian. We had a good conversation and afterwards he asked me for my number. When I wrote my name on the paper, he said that my last name was going to be his name. That was the first clue that he was going to be trouble. I tried to give him a chance, though. Oh, I forgot to mention that he was a deacon. The next day, he sent me a message talking about how much he liked me, and that God told him I was going to be his wife. I am pretty sure that if God told him that information, he would have also given that word to me. God didn't tell me that. So, I'm sure that didn't come from God! For three to four days he would send me messages about how we were going to be together and what he wanted to do to me. He was starting to make me nervous. He kept asking to come over but would never ask to take me out. He said he didn't have time to take me out. My response was, "If you don't have time to take me out, then you don't have time to come over to my house!" Shortly after that, the calls stopped. After these experiences, I had that conversation with God saying that I was done with relationships. I just didn't have time for the foolishness these guys were displaying. Just because I was divorced did not mean that I was desperate. After these dating fiascoes, I was done with dating.

In March of 2016, God blessed me to move out of my townhouse and into a beautiful ranch- style house on an acre of land. I bought the house with the intention of it just being me and possibly my

Divorced...NOT Devastated

future adopted child. In April of 2016, I had a conversation with my cousin, Kortney about dating and how she needed to get out and meet people. She started laughing and told me I needed to do the same thing. She told me that I couldn't tell her to get out and meet people, when I had decided to give up on dating. Yes, I guess she had a point, but I really wasn't interested in meeting new people. Reluctantly, I decided to give it another try. My friend, Ty invited me to a day party that the Omegas and my Sorority sisters, the ladies of Alpha Kappa Alpha Sorority, Inc. were having. I decided to go to the party. I really enjoyed myself at the party. I ended up meeting a nice guy who happened to be a member of Kappa Alpha Psi. I decided to give him five minutes because he approached me differently than the rest. He asked me to dance, but he also was having an actual conversation with me. Not just the, "Hey girl, what is your name? What is your sign? Do you come here often? Can I get your number?" type of banter, that dudes throw out, but an actual conversation. He was trying to get to know things about me that mattered and as a result, I became inquisitive and wanted to know more about him.

So, even though I had met a nice guy, things weren't always peaches and cream. I still had a lot of baggage from my divorce and past unhealthy relationships. I didn't make it easy for him. There is a song by Wale called, *Sabotage*. One of the lines in the song says, "My girl likes to sabotage our love." Yes, that was definitely me. I was arguing over any and everything. The years of unhealthy relationships caused me to struggle with functioning in a healthy relationship. I was making this new guy pay for the past pain that others had caused me. One day, he just sat

Divorced...NOT Devastated

me down and asked me why I was so angry all the time. He told me that he wasn't the enemy and that he wasn't trying to hurt me. He shared that he also wasn't interested in fighting with me. That conversation which happened two months into our relationship, showed me that he really did care. He could have just chosen to leave and say that it wasn't worth it; but he didn't leave. I wish I could say that was the end of my past causing problems in my present, but it wasn't. Honestly, it has taken a long time, and a lot of prayer and self- reflection before I could really let go of the past and fully embrace my present.

After working through the trust issues and anger, the next issue I had to tackle was my emotions. Being a Gemini, crazy emotions is a part of the territory. What I realized is that my emotions were causing a problem in my relationship. Now, I am not saying he was doing everything perfectly, but he was honestly trying, and he treated me well. What people don't understand is when you have been in unhealthy relationships for an extended time, you basically develop Post Traumatic Stress Disorder (PTSD). Certain things trigger and cause you to react in ways that don't seem rational to other people. This is what I was dealing with. Small things would trigger huge emotional reactions from me. Once I realized the issue, I began to pray about it and asked God to help me control my emotions. God speaks to me in a variety of ways. I began to read and hear messages from various sources about controlling emotions and how not being in control of your emotions can cause you to destroy relationships and block your blessings. My friend, Mrs. Gray called me unexpectedly one day and told me that she wanted to go to the Christian

Divorced...NOT Devastated

bookstore after our lunch date. As soon as she said it, I knew that God had something for me at the bookstore. We started walking in the store and she said just pick up whatever you want. Shortly after getting into the store, I saw a book called, *How Do I Deal with my Emotions*. I started laughing and said, "I see why we came here and I don't need anything else!" Once I started getting control of my emotions, things started changing for the better.

I also asked God to show me my partner's heart. I wanted to make sure that he had good intentions for me. I felt that his intentions were pure, but I wanted to know for sure. Only God could show me his true intentions. Once I prayed that prayer, things really started improving. Every time I turned around, this man was doing special things for me. It was quite amazing. Coming from years of unhealthy relationships to being with someone who truly cares for you is an adjustment; but one worth making! I don't know how this relationship is going to end, but for right now, I am enjoying the moment. I know that God brought him into my life for a reason. This relationship has helped me grow into a better person and this unique man is continuing to be a blessing to me. For that, I am thankful.

There is a quote that sums up what I have learned during this journey. "The secret of change is to focus all of your energy, not on fighting the old, but building the new." The quote is from *The Way of Peace Warrior,* by Dan Millman.

Divorced...NOT Devastated

Words of Wisdom

1. Make sure your partner is a God-fearing man. He doesn't have to go to church all the time, but he should have a relationship with God. When things get tough, you two will need to be able to go to God together. I heard a saying once that said, 'A man should be able to pray over more than just a plate of food.'

2. Pay close attention to the people he hangs around. Birds of a feather flock together. You can learn a lot about a person by the people closest to him.

3. Give yourself time to heal between relationships. You don't want to ruin a good thing, by not being mentally, emotionally, or spiritually ready. You can't make him pay for the sins of another man.

4. It is better to be single, than to be in an unhealthy relationship. Don't make anyone a priority, if they are making you an option.

5. God has placed everything inside of you that you need. Know that you are enough.

6. Do not to allow your past to dictate your future. If you choose not to let the past go, you can carry that baggage with you into every relationship. Leave the past in the past.

7. Learn from the past and let that lesson help you grow into a better person, not a bitter person.

8. Draw closer to God. You need God more than you need that man. Without God, the relationship or marriage will not last.

9. Enjoy your singleness. Focus on being the best version of yourself and when that man comes to find you, you will be ready. Ready, meaning- secure in yourself; complete and emotionally free from baggage.

10. Don't put God into a box. His vision is bigger than yours. The blessing that he has for you may not look the way you want. If you are one of those that has a checklist of items that your future mate must have, and that list is pages long, you may want to consider revising that list. Your non-negotiables should be characteristics like God-Fearing, Possessing Integrity, Family-Oriented, Stable, Secure in Himself, not things like over 6-feet, must make 6 figures, drives a nice car or any other materialistic items. The man that makes six figures may work long hours and may not have much time to spend with you. If your love language is quality time, then that will not work for you. 1 Samuel 16:7 says: *But the Lord said unto Samuel, Look not on his countenance, or on the height of his stature; because I have refused him; for the Lord seeth not as man seeth; for man looketh on the outward appearance, but the Lord looketh on the heart.* A person's character is God's priority. He qualifies the unqualified. He chooses people that we wouldn't choose. We tend to focus too much on the outside, but God wants us to focus on the inside. Wait on the man that God has prepared for

Divorced...NOT Devastated

you. Don't try to make it happen on your own. It is better to have 5 years with a godly man, than 25 years with a hellish one.

11. This is the most important thing that I have learned during my relationship- We need to love each other like Jesus loves. During a conversation, my friend told me that I needed to read Corinthians again and that moment changed everything. 1 Corinthians 13:4-7 says, *Love is patient, love is kind. It does not envy, it does not boast, it is not proud. It does not dishonor others, it is not self-seeking, it is not easily angered, it keeps no record of wrongs. Love does not delight in evil but rejoices with the truth. It always protects, always trusts, always hopes, always perseveres.*

As I read this verse again, it brought tears to my eyes, because I realized in that moment that I had been saying things that were not said in love. This man didn't deserve that. I decided, in that moment that I needed to do better. If you are saying things to your partner that dishonors him or her, you are not showing love. If you are telling your partner that what they are doing isn't enough, when they are doing all they can, that isn't love. If everything you are doing or saying is based on what is good for you, that isn't love. If you are constantly bringing up past things that they have done wrong, that isn't love. Keep 1 Corinthians 13 close to your heart and you will always know that you are showing genuine love to your partner.

My Prayer for You

It is not by chance that you picked up this book, it was by God's guidance. My prayer for you is that something in my chapter has touched your heart, mind, and spirit. If you are suffering from bitterness, shame, guilt, depression, or anger from your past, I bind and cast out those spirits in the name of Jesus. Our Father said that you are fearfully and wonderfully made. He has forgiven you and you must forgive yourself. Everything that you went through wasn't to hurt or harm you; it was to prepare and grow you. You can't have an effective testimony, if there has been no test. Someone will need the wisdom that you have received through your test. Be ready to share when the time is right. I pray that God sends people in your life that will build you up and not tear you down. If you have given up on love, I pray that God touches your heart and allows you to have an open heart that can give and receive love. 1 Corinthians 13:13 says, 'And now these three remain: Hope, Faith and Love. But the greatest of these is love.' Always remember that Jesus loves you just as you are. You are enough.

In the matchless name of Jesus, Amen.

Author Tonza Ruffin

Tonza Ruffin

A graduate of East Carolina University, Tonza D. Ruffin earned her B.A. in Political Science with a minor in Women's Studies. She went on to earn her Juris Doctorate Degree from Georgia State University College of Law. After being admitted to the North Carolina Bar, Tonza began her career, more than seventeen years ago, as an attorney in Eastern North Carolina where she has dedicated her career to defending individuals charged with crimes that range from minor misdemeanor offenses to capital murder.

Approximately two years ago, Tonza decided to pursue her passion for writing and began her blog- *SouthernMomJD*. *SouthernMomJD* is filled with many heartfelt, funny, and transparent stories about Tonza's journey as a southern woman, southern lawyer, and southern mom.

Recently, Tonza began writing as a columnist for her hometown newspaper, the *Bertie-Ledger Advance*. In addition to her passion for writing and advocacy, Tonza currently serves on the boards of KIPP ENC(Knowledge is Power Program, Eastern North Carolina) and the Center for Death Penalty Litigation.

Tonza's most important accomplishment...she is the proud mother of three beautiful girls.

If I Were To Be Honest

If I were to be honest, I knew that my husband and I never should have been together in the first place. If I were to be honest, I would tell you that my decision to go out with him, and, enter into a twelve-year relationship had very little to do with my own thoughts and feelings. If I were to be honest, I would tell you that I was not strong enough back then to fight against the societal messages that were being fed to me regularly.

Me, the woman who chose to live in an area that left me starving for a life-fulfilled. Me, the woman who clearly failed in the area of relationships. Me, the single mother of two beautiful girls, who could not manage to keep their father in their lives.

If I were to be honest…

I returned to eastern North Carolina to practice law nineteen years ago. Eastern North Carolina was not my first, or, last choice. In fact, it wasn't a choice at all. In my mind, I was supposed to be a jet setter, traveling around the world, living a life full of fun and adventure. In my reality, I was the twenty-nine-year-old, single mother of two girls, one a newborn, and I had just completed law school and needed to provide

Divorced...NOT Devastated

stability and security for these children that I chose to bring into this world.

      Heartbroken and disappointed, I packed my bags and returned "home". My desire for mental stimulation and worldwide experiences was outweighed by my need to have my village surrounding me during this next chapter in my life. I needed a support system to ensure that my babies would be loved and taken care of as I worked incessantly to ensure financial stability for us. You see, having my oldest daughter when I was only nineteen years old triggered a fear of failure in me like no other. I constantly felt suffocated by the statistics and the societal judgment that concluded, my child and I, were destined for a life of poverty. Each day, after her birth, I reminded myself that I had made the decision to bring this girl child in the world at a time when I was still a girl child myself, but, I owed her a life where she was not marginalized by my decision to be a teen mother. As a result, with a lot of grit, determination, and support, I completed my undergraduate degree and went on to obtain my Juris Doctorate. Once sworn into the practice of law, I became obsessed with being the best litigator that I could be. Simply put, I was a "workaholic" whose entire focus was on creating financial stability and security for me and my children. As for love, I limited myself to what felt safe and did not interfere with my career goals.

      After years of dedicating my life to my career and my children, I developed a desire to experience love outside of the safe parameters that I had set for myself. I met my husband at an annual Christmas party. He was new to our crowd and appeared to have an air of confidence that I

Divorced...NOT Devastated

had not seen in a while. What I mistook for machismo later revealed itself as the mask he used to hide all of his insecurities. What I mistook for charming persistence later revealed itself as a desire to control.

I agreed, reluctantly, to go out on a date with him. Despite the fact that my "inner voice" quickly let me know that he was not for me, I stubbornly questioned why he couldn't "become" the one for me. You see, this "successful" African-American woman yearned to check one more box, *a successful relationship filled with passion and love*. So instead of listening to the vibrations in my spirit that said, "he is not the one", I chastised myself for not being appreciative to the gods for sending me this man. I convinced myself that this relationship could be successful if I worked hard at making it a success. After all, hard work and determination had worked in every other aspect of my life, why couldn't it work in love?

We quickly began living together and thus the downward spiral began. I soon realized that my personality caused quite a stir in my future husband. In hindsight, I believe that my passive acceptance of our relationship gave him the signal that I was looking for a savior. And, maybe I was. So, he was caught off guard, to say the least, when I dared to voice my opinions (quite strongly I must say), and resist the notion of him being the head of the household. The constant tug of war for control eventually led to a lot of screaming, yelling, and downright verbal abuse on our part. To say my home became a toxic cesspool of anger and resentment is an understatement.

Divorced...NOT Devastated

Eventually the verbal abuse escalated to physical abuse. By then, I was immersed in the "societal cover up" which said, no matter how bad it is behind closed doors, one must always put a smile on their face, and present to the world as though their life is perfect. Never put your business out in the streets because people will use that against you. When the toxicity in our household flowed over into our public lives, I was forced to take off the mask. I mean, how does one keep the fraud up when you are unable to contain your anger and resentment in front of people? More importantly, how does one continue to participate in the "societal cover up" when you are wearing a black eye for the whole world to see?

If I were to be honest, I would tell you that the physical abuse did not make me leave. Ironically, my efforts to prove that I was too strong to be broken by this verbally and physically abusive man led to me spewing venom and lashing out physically on a few occasions myself. Despite all of the turmoil that existed in our home, we selfishly decided to bring another child into the world. Now, the mother of three girls, I was more determined to make this toxic, unhealthy relationship work because, selfishly, my focus was on my desire to "successfully" raise a child in a two-parent household. Being directed and influenced by societal standards of what my life should look like as a professional Black woman, I continued, despite the turmoil and abuse, to try to turn this chapter of my life around, so that it would end with us growing old together, looking back at our tumultuous times, and saying to one another, "we made it!" Fortunately, my spirit had already decided that I was not going to spend the rest of my life "trying to make chicken salad out of chicken shit", as the old folks used to say.

It took me approximately two years of deep reflection, sadness, and contemplation before I gained the courage to leave my marriage. When I finally made the decision to leave, I was able to say with a clear conscious, "I don't give a damn what society says! I am NOT happy! And, I DESERVE to be happy!"

Although I knew with every fiber of my being that ending my marriage was the right thing to do, my husband did not make it easy for me. While I wanted to remain in our home so that the children could maintain some stability, he refused to entertain any thought of me keeping the marital home. Struggling with the thought of uprooting my children toward the end of the school year made me second guess that strong voice inside of me saying, "you got this girl". Knowing that if I fought to stay in the home, I would deplete the energy I mustered up to leave, I threw a few items in a U-Haul. and returned to my hometown to begin to rebuild my life.

As much as I would like to blame him for everything that went wrong and caused us to go our separate ways, the reality is, because I refused to listen to my inner spirit, I committed to a relationship that I was unable to truly commit to. And, despite his best efforts, my husband knew that my heart was not in it. So, we spent twelve years exhibiting Black Love for the world instead of being true to ourselves.

Divorced...NOT Devastated

It has been two years since I left my marriage. It has been one year since I have been divorced. While the transition was not easy, I can truly say that it was well worth it. I have grown so much as a woman since making this most important decision. Twenty years ago, I would be going to great lengths to prove to the world that I don't need a man. Today I have let go of the weight of proving anything to the world and center my energy around figuring out what makes me happy. While, I welcome the idea of sharing my life with another, I am also very comfortable with being alone. My focus is truly on living a life fulfilled and listening to my inner voice. My goal is to have no regrets and to find the beauty in this wonderful gift of life that I have been given.

I am now in a loving relationship. If I were to be honest, I thought I was all "healed up" when I began this new experience, until I began to feel the anger and rage from my past come back into the picture. In my piece, <u>The Shift</u>, I wrote:

> I found myself in a constant state of anger, always ready for war. Taking the easy way out, I blamed my raging hormones and accepted that this was something I had to endure and manage through *medication, meditation, and mindfulness*. Unable to shake the feeling of defeat at the thought of taking medication, I immersed myself into the world of meditation and mindfulness. I listened to every empowerment speech I could listen to. I found a quiet place and began to meditate and center myself in the mornings. I worked to constantly bring myself back to the present when my mind wandered to the things that ignited that fire inside of me. And, while these practices were extremely helpful at allowing me to grow as a person, they did not completely quell the rage that would surface when I felt wronged.

Divorced...NOT Devastated

Continuing to search for affirmation, I began to lean on my woman circle. *Was I wrong for feeling the way I felt? Am I crazy for thinking there is something wrong with this scenario? What am I doing wrong?*

While most of my circle agreed that my concerns were valid, the consensus was that I needed to focus my energy on the storm inside of me. With that in mind, the advice was for me to "fall back". Don't make yourself so available and willing to do whatever a man wants you to do. Men love a challenge and you need to give it to them or they will lose interest. More importantly, "falling back" would give me the time I needed to calm the storm.

Priding myself on no longer playing games, I could not bring myself to "fall back". I didn't believe the answer was for me to act as though I wasn't bothered when in fact I was. Everything about that notion just felt wrong to me.

And then it happened. As I sat there disappointed and alone with my thoughts, *the shift occurred.* I realized that I was raging outwardly, but, I was the person that I was truly angry with. I was angry because I was tackling my relationships like I did my career, my life as a mom, my life as a writer, blogger, homeowner, etc. I was putting in a lot of work believing that my work would automatically lead to a successful relationship, *i.e. my significant other would love me, appreciate me, choose me.* Quite frankly, this "work hard" mindset had left me burned out mentally and emotionally which manifested itself in the form of rage.

With all of my energy being directed at working so hard to make sure my significant other knew I was worthy, I had failed to spend any time thinking about, whether or not my significant other was worthy of the love that I had to give. I never thought about whether or not my significant other was capable of truly appreciating me. I never thought about whether or not my significant other was treating me with the love and respect that I

Divorced...NOT Devastated

deserved. Or, even able to treat me with the love and respect that I deserved. In my mind, I held on to the false and exhausting belief that all of that depended on me.

While the shift came about as a result of another disappointing experience, I am no longer resentful. Sometimes we have to learn lessons the hard way. This shift has allowed me to rid myself of the burden of being the caretaker for relationships. I am no longer angry and resentful because I no longer take on the burden of proving that I am worthy of love. I have hit the reset button and am focused on living my best life, and with that, the anger and rage has subsided. Of course, I am human which means I cannot guarantee a life void of anger. But, with awareness and growth comes my ability to reset as needed.

My style of parenting looks very different these days as well. I drove my first two children to excellence, and probably some neurosis, because, if I were to be honest, I was obsessed with dispelling the myth that teen mom = poverty. I was selfish, and concerned about how their actions were a reflection of me. Again, letting that "societal noise" lead me, instead of my "inner spirit". And, while I am being honest, they also benefited, materially, from the guilt I felt about exposing them to what I knew to be unhealthy relationships. Because I was struggling with my brokenness, it was easier to provide "things" rather than engage in those tough conversations that would lead to peace, healing, and happiness.

Today, I have created a space where we deal with the good, the bad, and the ugly. I talk about the tough stuff and try to be present and completely tuned in when they are sharing with me. While it is not always

Divorced…NOT Devastated

easy to hear my children talk to me about the pain I may have caused for them, I prefer them talking to me, rather than engage in self-destructive behavior because they are silenced by the fear of expressing themselves. Of course, my home is normal in that, many times, my teenager will look at me with the side eye when I am in my period of reflection and sharing ☺. My oldest daughter will laugh uncontrollably when I am in my "mother earth" mode. And, my youngest will look at me as though I am crazy when I am trying to talk when her only concern is how long I am going to let her play Xbox that night.

I am hoping that in the years to come I can help to repair some of the damage I may have done with my older girls. I am hopeful that my youngest will bypass that phase of punishing herself by trying to fit into the societal mold of who she should be. This doesn't mean that I have let go of my desire for my children to be "excellent", but, I now realize that excellence means nothing if your self-esteem doesn't even allow you to see, and, embrace your excellence.

If I could sit down and enjoy a cup of coffee with you, I would share these things I learned from my journey:

Find your inner voice. We all have one! All you have to do is take the time to connect, be honest, and get to know yourself and then you will begin to hear that inner voice speaking to you.

Listen to your inner voice. Listen, Listen, Listen! Be quiet, and, listen to your inner voice. When you feel the pressure of trying to fit into the mold of what society has in store for you, take a step back and listen. When your inner voice is guiding you in a direction that might make others uncomfortable, listen. You will find yourself able to flourish and be happy without a lot of obstacles, if you just listen.

<u>Let that ego go</u>. Our egos will be the death of us if we do not check them at the door. It was my ego that forced me to ignore the vibrations in my spirit. My ego allowed me to naively believe that hard work on my part was the key to a successful relationship.

My ego was a cover up for the fact that I was not in love with myself.

When I was able to let my ego go, I was able to smile from the inside out and truly be happy in the moment.

<u>DO NOT participate in the "societal cover up"</u>. I will let you in on a little secret, society is going to talk and judge regardless of what you do. So, why not be true to yourself and live your best life?

I will let you in on another secret. We are not really good at the "societal cover up". Your energy lets people know when things are not quite right in your life. It is only because they do not want to interfere in your pain that we walk around, falsely, believing that we are succeeding at the cover up.

So, let your guard down. It is okay to be real with yourself.

Divorced...NOT Devastated

<u>Love you</u>. Self-love and self-care have got to become a priority in your life. Self-love involves embracing all of you. Stop beating yourself up for the things you do not like about yourself. None of us are perfect. Embrace being "perfectly imperfect", a term I heard on my favorite television show, "This is Us".

> "I've changed.
> Irrevocably.
> Permanently.
> My soul is richer and my heart is fuller in brokenness than it ever was without. I've learned true despair, and it's made me learn to appreciate true joy."
>
> — Lexi Behrndt

Author Errico Moore

Errico Moore

Errico Renee Moore, M.P.A is an Alumni of Strayer University, where she received her Bachelor's Degree in Business Administration and her Master's Degree in Public Administration. She is the founder of Moore Inspirations. Moore Inspirations serves the purpose of uplifting and encouraging others through the word of God and prayer. She feels that her purpose in life is to use her voice to edify and promote God's Awesomeness; whether it be formal or informal. Errico loves encouraging God's people through song, word, and prayer. To sum it all up- she is just a country girl who loves to have fun and tell people about the goodness of God!

She is the wife of Roderick Moore and the mother of daughter, Rmani Henry and her fur baby, Cannon Moore. Her mother Armeta Graham is a big inspiration in her life. The late John Graham IV, her big brother played a major role in shaping and molding her into the person that she is today. Errico is currently employed with the North Carolina Department of Motor Vehicles where she serves as a Staff Development Specialist. She has been with the division for fifteen years and loves serving the citizens of North Carolina. Errico is also, the owner of Travel Moore that she just launched in December of 2017 to assist all who enjoy traveling the world!

Errico hopes there is something shared in her chapter that will encourage someone who is going through or went through a situation similar to hers to believe in their capacity to overcome. She will leave you with two scriptures that helped her along her journey.

Psalm 30:5 King James Version (KJV)

5 For his anger endureth but a moment; in his favour is life: weeping may endure for a night, but joy cometh in the morning.

Proverbs 3:5-6 New International Version (NIV)

5 Trust in the LORD with all your heart and lean not on your own understanding;
6 in all your ways submit to him, and he will make your paths straight .

It Ain't Over

By: Maurette Brown Clark

It Ain't Over

I know the odds look stacked against you

And it seems there's no way out

I know the issue seems unchangeable

And that there's no reason to shout

But the impossible is God's chance

To work a miracle, a miracle

So just know

It ain't over until God says it's over

It ain't over until God says it's done

It ain't over until God says it's over

Keep fighting until your victory is won

He never said it would be easy

But you're a winner in the end

Jesus defeated all your enemies

Way before the fight began

But the impossible is God's chance

To work a miracle, a miracle

So just know

It ain't over until God says it's over

It ain't over until God says it's done

It ain't over until God says it's over

Keep fighting until your victory is won.

The Preacher's Son

I*t ain't over until God says it's over,* is what I kept telling myself while going through a major disappointment. I found myself singing the verses to this very song; believing that restoration would come to my marriage. However, the truth is my marriage was over before it began.

My dream man, Peter and I met in May of 1993 through a mutual friend. We never really had a steady relationship until the spring of 2000. We were off and on for about 7 years before we were in a committed relationship. During those years it didn't matter to me who was in my life at the time. When Peter came around he took precedence, because to me, he was my dream man. I loved his character and he was just an all-around type guy. He could adapt to any situation. Peter was a preacher's kid who went to church and he was the first guy that I ever dated that had one or more church suits! I was so impressed to be with a guy who went to church and dressed the part. When we came back into each other's lives in 2000, I had just lost my brother to a car accident and Peter was just getting out of another relationship. It was nothing for him and I to go a period of time and reconnect. That's how our relationship was since 1993, however this time it grew into a committed relationship.

Divorced...NOT Devastated

On February 14th, 2002, I thought I had succeeded in marrying the man of my dreams. We had a beautiful island wedding. We were married in Montego Bay Jamaica at the Sandals Resort. We enjoyed our wedding and honeymoon with just the two of us. This was the beginning of our happy life together, as a married couple, or so I thought. Once we returned home, we had a formal reception for our families and friends in our hometown. It was at our reception that my husband's mistress decided to attend and celebrate with us!

How many of you know that the man that you date is the same man that you marry? Once you are married things don't change. Common sense, right? However, my common sense did not kick in and tell me – "if you knew deep down that he was being unfaithful during the engagement, you knew he would do the same thing during the marriage." We had attended pre- marital counseling and I thought it was clear to both of us what God expected between husband and wife. My expectations were that we would be a family that served God and lived according to His plan. I took our vows seriously. I believed Peter when he said that he would be my loving and faithful husband, in sickness and in health, as long as we both shall live." So many times, it had been prophesied to us that it was God's will for us to be married. Even during our troubled times, it was prophesied that he was the man that God had for me.

I expected my husband to love me as Christ loves the church and put me first. This was difficult for him, because he came from a very

Divorced...NOT Devastated

close-knit family. I understood the conflict and reasoned that his family was there before me. The love and involvement he had for his family were characteristics that I admired, and that had drawn me close to him. I think learning how to be the head of our household and still be what his family was used to him being for them, became challenging for the both of us. Separation began to creep in between us as my suspicions of his infidelity grew. I did not always want to be around, especially since the "other woman" attended every family event! I can remember talking to my aunt about the situation and she told me that- "you stick by your husband no matter what." My aunt and uncle were married for over 40 years; separated only when my uncle died. My aunt shared with me that her husband had made some bad choices in their marriage and even had outside children. She explained that she stayed with her husband because of her vow to Christ. I valued her opinion but did not feel that it was a situation that I could handle.

Maya Angelou says it best- "When someone shows you who they are, believe them the first time". During the first months of being married, the same patterns continued. He was always staying at his parents' house to be closer to his job. I thought that was understandable because he was a truck driver and depending upon where he was loading and unloading, his parents' house might be more convenient. However, I knew something wasn't right, because I would call him certain times at night and he wouldn't answer. Then, I would call his parents' house and he would not be there. I would question him about the situation and he

Divorced...NOT Devastated

would assure me that everything was cool. He said he was hanging out with his friends and didn't hear my call or he was asleep.

This continued on and off for a year or more. I complained to my friends and they told me- "you are just going through growing pains and you will get through it." Emotional pain became a familiar feeling for me; so, I became numb to the situation. I believed that if I ignored the rumors and the suspicions, it would all go away. I grew up in the church believing that whatever you ask God for in prayer, it would be given. Things began to change for the better; we purchased our home on our first anniversary. September of 2003, we revisited Montego Bay to be a witness for one of my girlfriend's wedding. All the memories of our wedding night came back to us and we made a vow to work on our marriage.

January of 2004, I found out that I was going to give birth to our first child. I was so excited to be having a child together with my husband! I had a good pregnancy and a good support team. Then, the rumors started resurfacing again concerning the same chic and she was back showing up at the family events, but I remained focused on giving birth to our child. I had a long conversation with myself and we agreed that once I had our child things were going to be done differently. I gave birth to our Sweet Angel in September, 2004.

Shortly after delivery, the old Peter started showing up again; not coming home or answering his phone. I was at the end of my ropes with this. I began to do what I knew to do and that was to pray." God, please

Divorced...NOT Devastated

fix my marriage because I do not want to be a single parent. I watched my mother do it for her children and that was not the desire I had for myself. I grew up without my father in the home and I didn't want the same for my child. I kept praying and praying, and the more I prayed, the worst things became.

When you live in an area where everyone knows everybody, news travels quickly. I began to hear rumors about Peter and a chic named Spice (the dispatcher) messing around. This was the same female that I had suspected prior to us getting married, but I had let it go at the time because she was married to a guy from the same community, in which they all lived. I confronted Peter about the rumors and he declared that they were not true. He swore to me that he was not cheating. We went to marriage counseling for about a month and he never confessed to having an extra- marital affair during the sessions. The counselor was convinced that he was not cheating, but I had a gut feeling within my soul that he was. The other woman would text him and I would respond back and her response would make me feel that I was the mistress and not the wife! Spice had the best of both worlds, a husband at home and my husband by day and night, as she desired. I would get into arguments about it with Peter and demand that he stop talking to her, but that didn't happen. I vowed that once I had my child I was not going to put up with him coming home all times of the night or not coming home at all; or his mistress calling his phone and texting day and night.

I began to stop searching for answers, confronting people about the situation, and always checking behind Peter. Instead I started asking

Divorced...NOT Devastated

God to show me what it was that he needed me to see and to free me from this life of uncertainty. Once I let go, and let God, things began to come to the forefront. Peter and Spice were being seen in public, and people would send me pictures, text me with information, and call me and tell me the specifics of their encounters. Against my promise to myself, I still confronted him with this information and he continued to deny it. One day I was cleaning up and going through the mail on the counter and there was my answer. A hotel coupon came to our address with her name on it, and a letter from a rental car company. Of course I was blamed for sending the coupon to our house. Really, I wanted my marriage to fall apart that bad? I called the rental car company and they gave me the dates that the car was rented, what city, how many miles it was driven and by whom.

I know you are wondering how I obtained all that confidential information. Well, let me tell you. Being a private investigator must have been my first calling! I just called the rental car company on behalf of our trucking company, seeking the information for auditing purposes and they gave me everything I needed! The dates that he rented the car for a trip to Georgia, he was supposed to be working in Georgia with his trucking company! That call confirmed the rumors of Peter and his mistress being in Georgia to visit her brother. That phone call pushed me to burn up his clothes on the sidewalk of our house and almost made me set that 18-wheeler on fire! Now, that would have been crazy, right?

After all the confirmations, the overt disrespect and him telling me that he didn't want to be married any longer, I was done! I finally

Divorced...NOT Devastated

accepted the fact that this was more than infidelity, this was mental and emotional abuse as well. I didn't have to take that any longer and made the final decision to separate.

"Weeping May Endure for A Night, but Joy Cometh in the Morning"

Not once did I stop and ask God what was his plan for my child; nor did I ask God-"where do I go from here?" I was still stuck on praying the prayer of restoration. On Resurrection Sunday 2005, I was at the altar receiving prayer, and the woman of God told me "It's going to get worse before it gets better; but God will carry you through this. I left the altar more confused than I was before I went to the altar. I didn't know if that was my confirmation that my situation was going to work out soon or that all Hell was going to break loose! I can tell you that things really did get worst for me emotionally. I was more concerned about what people were going to say and think about me than the reality of the matter. Once I told my mother about the reasons for the separation, which to my surprised she already knew, I felt better. I developed the mindset that I had to do what was best for my small child and myself. I had a good support team which included my close family, my best friend, and my church family. I was very active in church; participating in the choir, praise team, young adult council and the program planning committees. This kept my mind off the situation. I began to seek God like never before for direction and his will for my life.

I was at the beginning of my new journey in life as a single mother and I must say, God blessed me through it all. Finances were an

Divorced...NOT Devastated

immediate concern. It was clear that I could not afford to maintain our house. I lived in the house for 7 months without paying the mortgage but when the house was sold, I received a check for thousands of dollars! I went to closing to sign off as the seller and to my surprise they gave me a check even though I owed them mortgage payments that totaled over $7500!

Selling my house and moving into an apartment was a release for me. My support system helped me move to my new apartment which was closer to my family and job. You would think after not paying the mortgage for that many months it would be hard to find an apartment because of credit issues. To the contrary, I was approved for a 2-bedroom townhouse fifteen minutes away from my job and 5 minutes away from my child's day care. I explained my situation to the leasing agent and she enrolled me in a program that enabled me to afford the rent with no money down and the first month's rent free! There were times when I looked at my check book and the bills and would just cry, because I didn't know how I was going to do it. I did not receive child support regularly, so I couldn't count on it. I spent many days at the Johnston County Court House fighting for child support to assist me in taking care of my child. Multiple court appointments required me to miss work. I can remember one day at court, PETER said to me that- "God rains on the unjust just as well as the just, so I will be alright." In those moments, God would speak to me; saying- "I am Jehovah Jireh, your provider." His promise was fulfilled. Every bill was met, nothing was cut off and we ate. We didn't have everything that we wanted but we had what we needed!

Divorced...NOT Devastated

Through it all, I still trusted, leaned, and depended upon God because at the end of the day that was all I had; God and my sweet angel. As time went by it became easier; the anger and the bitterness went away. There were times I would be out in public and see the two of them together. Yes, Peter and the same woman who he insisted that he was not having an affair with, and it would bother me but I knew that God had greater for me.

In August of 2007, at a Women's Retreat, a prophetess prayed over me. I cannot remember anything that was said except, "Lord prepare her for the true husband that you have for her". This gave me a hope and a desire for love again. Upon leaving the conference, a lady approached me with a check, saying that she wanted to sow into my life by paying for my divorce! I was holding on to what I thought would be a restoration of my marriage, but this moment in time, was the beginning of a new focus. Monday Morning, when I returned to Raleigh, without hesitation, I went to file for my divorce!

Once my divorce was final, I felt free and optimistic. This opened up the idea of dating again. Yet, once I stepped out into the dating arena, it was not all that it was cracked up to be. I discovered that I truly was not ready. I still had issues from my past hurts that would not allow me to fully open up to another person. I found myself in situations where I was in and out of relationships. I even dated a married man for some time, convinced that he would leave his wife for me. How did I end up in that situation, knowing that when it was done to me, it destroyed my family and caused me great pain? I don't know, but it gave me a deeper

Divorced...NOT Devastated

understanding of what happened in my marriage. Previously, I had felt that anyone who dated a married person was the worst person ever. Yet, here I was caught up in the same situation. I learned to never say what you will not do in life because you might find yourself doing the very same thing that you swore against.

July 19, 2010; I remember this day so clearly. I was having a regular conversation with God, one morning as I was getting my daughter ready for school. I said aloud, "God please send me a husband that is willing to be a father for my child, because I am so tired of going to school functions alone and everybody looking at me like-'does this child have a father.' I reminded Him of the prayer at the retreat in 2007, as well as my repentance for my wrong doings. Then I ended my conversation by saying- "so God if you are up there listening to me, I am ready for my God-sent husband". Then, my Sweet Angel said to me, "Mommy are you talking to God again"? I replied, "yes, baby and he is going to answer mommy's prayers soon."

When I tell you, it doesn't take long when God is in it, please believe just that! On July 23, 2010, I received a text from my best friend's husband; asking me to give him a call. I immediately called him back and he asked if I was dating anyone because he had a friend that had seen my picture on Facebook and was interested in meeting me. Inquisitive, I started asking him questions like- "who is this friend?" Then I began to name some guys that I knew were friends of his. He answered, "no" to all the friends that I named, so I said, "what is his name?" He said, Pete, and I replied, "what is his full name?" He said "Peter". I shook my head in

Divorced...NOT Devastated

disbelief! I said, "nope, I am not interested! He has the *same* name as my ex, nope! Look at God with his faithful self! My friend said, "you cannot count the man out because of his name. Just talk to him." So, I agreed to talk with Peter on the phone and I played the 20 questions game with him. I found out a lot in those 20 questions; like his and my ex's birthdays are 2 days apart. I am convinced that God really has a sense of humor! I had no idea that phone call would become the start of a friendship that would lead to a wonderful marriage. We talked on the phone for a week and decided that we wanted to meet in person.

I had a church event back home that following weekend. I was so excited to meet this guy that I left a day earlier than what was planned. It was in the Walgreens parking lot in Leland, NC where I met my King for the first time. Peter and I went on our first date that weekend and I knew it was something special about this guy. We talked about where we were in life and where we would like to be in the future. The day Sweet Angel met him, she asked him just as many questions as I did during our first telephone conversation. She questioned- "do you have a job? Do you have a car?" She had to make sure he was right for her mommy. It was hard for me to trust again and it caused problems for Peter and I in the beginning of our relationship. It felt as if I couldn't let go of the past hurt and trust another man with my heart. I can recall Peter telling me," you have to give me a chance to prove to you who I am and not punish me for what another man has done to you in the past." My daughter would say to me, "Mommy, who hurt you so bad that you can't trust people"

Divorced...NOT Devastated

and it really began to sink in that I had to let go of the past to move into our future.

When Peter and I met, I was in school completing my bachelor's degree and he lived in another city. Long distance relationships can be hard but that was not the case with us. It allowed us time to flourish in other areas of our lives. We both were single parents with jobs and hobbies that took priority in our lives, but we still made time for us. There were times when Sweet Angel would call him and invite him to dinner on Sundays, if she hadn't seen him for a couple of weeks. He would show up at the door and I would be surprised because we talked earlier and he knew that I was going to use that as a study day. I would look at Sweet Angel and she would say, "I haven't seen him in a long time so I invited him to eat dinner and watch a movie with *me*." It was apparent that she had begun to view him as a significant person in our lives.

In December of 2010, I completed my bachelor's degree with honors, and the next week closed on my new house. As I conclude this chapter, I would like to leave you with this thought "If God said it, believe it and watch it come to pass". It was prophesied to me that God would give me *double for my trouble*; well I can say that he gave me *triple for my trouble*. On December 21, 2010, Peter and I were united in holy matrimony and became one. Some people said that I was crazy for marrying someone I only knew for 5 months, but what God said overrides what people say. Don't get me wrong, we had our share of problems, but we knew that with God there was nothing too hard for us to work out. I knew this was the true husband that was prayed for at the

Divorced…NOT Devastated

Women's Conference. God really showed his sense of humor when he prepared another *husband* for me; but I must say that he did some of his best work on *this* man! He is an awesome Man of God that takes his role as King of his Castle very seriously. He is faithful and shows his commitment to our family through his daily actions.

At the time, when I was going through turmoil in my first marriage, I couldn't see that God was setting me up for something bigger in life. I can truly say that I don't regret anything that has taken place in my life because I would not be who I am today if I had not gone through what I went through. My first husband and I have a good parenting relationship. We have set aside our differences and become the effective parents for our child. The most important thing that I realized, is that you will reap what you sow. God has a way to bring your wrongs back to your memory. There were times in my life when I interfered in others' relationships, knowing that it was wrong. So, my *reaping* came back to me, unfortunately not through a casual relationship, but through my first marriage. As I share with you my life experiences, know that I was devastated at the time of the separation but now, I can say that I have not only triumphed over my situation, but I have grown to be a strong woman of God. I use my life experiences to encourage others that there is a bright side and that God is no respecter of persons. If he brought me through; he will do the same thing for you. Life does not end because of a divorce; it was the beginning of a new journey for me. If I had not gone through a divorce I would not have met my Awesome Husband, Roderick Moore

Divorced...NOT Devastated

(actual name), who loves and cherishes me and our children! Therefore, I am divorced...NOT devastated! I am BLESSED!

LaKesha Lakes

Divorced...NOT Devastated

LaKesha Lakes

Kesha Lakes is a woman of determination and perseverance. From Muskegon Heights, Michigan, Kesha had to take on the reigns of responsibility at the early age of 20, when she became the mother of her daughter, Mieya. Kesha attended Baker College, pursuing an Elementary Education degree. She went on to work in the school system for over three years as a pre-kindergarten administrative assistant. During this time, Kesha became the mother of a second daughter, Jade. While working in education, Kesha loved being surrounded by children daily. Kesha has a true heart for kids and loved to see a child's special gifts recognized.

Kesha didn't stop there; she became an entrepreneur by starting her own children's dress boutique called "Day Dreams." While attempting to move clothing inventory from the fashion districts of New York and Los Angeles, a dear friend told Kesha that a job with the airlines might be of great benefit to her, both personally and for her business. Kesha was introduced to the position of flight attendant and was hired by Continental Airlines. She immediately had a passion for traveling, while also accruing products for her boutique with ease.

While Kesha started her airline career to benefit her business, she went on to enjoy an over 10-year career with Continental/United Airlines. Kesha relished in serving first-time fliers, making their voyage one of ease and enjoyment. Kesha has traveled to over 22 countries and over 150 major cities outside the US.

Kesha's airline career came to a sudden end as she faced extraordinary personal and health crises. During this time, God revealed Kesha's true strength, as well as lessons that she is determined to share with other young mothers. Currently, Kesha is developing her own organization for young mothers, called Young M.O.M.S. (Motivating Objectives to Manifest Success). Kesha wants to help young mothers to know that having a baby does not have to stop them from achieving goals and they can be confident and productive citizens.

Kesha has recently returned to her amazing flight career and is focused more than ever on the things that matter in life - her daughters, enjoying life daily, and pursuing her goals and dreams of comforting others.

Provoked Pain

In December of 2009 I was on the run from an abusive relationship in Pennsylvania. In that same month Trevor (the name we'll use for my ex-husband) had been released from a 7 year prison sentence. Our reunion occurred at my sister's birthday party where all of our friends were shocked, yet excited to see us in the same room. Even my mother and father were happy to see him. That night he bet his friends that he could make me his wife and I was so excited to see him as a free man that I gave him all of my attention. I even kicked everyone out of the VIP section that my sister had reserved so we could catch up without interruption.

See, he and I had dated in middle school and a small portion of high school. We used to have so much fun! We were kind of a big deal because he had a car, or at least he was licensed to drive his disabled mother's car. We stood out amongst the other students because at such a young age, he used to pick me up from cheer leading practice and drive me home. We were known for being advanced honor students and both of us were great athletes, too. Now, all these years later, we still had the same groups of friends and they ALL wanted to see us back together.

Divorced...NOT Devastated

Without pressure from outsiders, we were dating in no time. I remember the very first time I picked him up for a date... halfway through the ride to our destination I had to pull over to allow him to throw up. I contributed it to nervousness but I knew he had been drinking in celebration of his freedom.

We had hood love, not to be misconstrued for ghetto love; we had a love that everyone from our neighborhood adored. We quickly rented a big ole house together and filled it with exclusive furniture and decorated all the rooms in a fashion that fascinated our never-ending parade of company. We had major issues from the start though: (1) I was off work on a nine month leave of absence and had to return soon, (2) He had seven years of catching up and *growing up* to do (3) We were in love with our fairy tale beginning and relied on it to see us through a relationship.

I'll fast forward through the many nights Trevor got drunk and all hell broke loose... all the times he resorted to spending the night elsewhere instead of coming home and the constant lying, cheating, going broke and other major indiscretions... Quite honestly, I didn't pay attention to ANY of it... I was in *Love*.

When it was time for me to go back to work, we both were absolutely elated. I was, once again, actually enjoying my love for flying and it gave Trevor the ability to brag on his "flight attendant" girlfriend. This also meant a steadier stream of income, as we both had been attending college. At first, he loved dropping me off at the airport and we

Divorced...NOT Devastated

had plenty of telephone conversations. Although he never pretended to sulk in my absence, he was absolutely happy when I got back from my flight assignments.

One day, upon my return to the house, in my slight O.C.D. awareness, I noticed a "cleaned" stain on the beige carpet near the living room sofa. This immediately sent me on investigation of the rest of the house. My intuition led me to find a few minor oddities that peaked my curiosity enough to question Trevor about what had happened in the house while I was at work. He lied. He said that one of my daughters must have spilled something and tried to get it up. I did not protest; I never did. But the girls had been with their dad the whole time. I didn't tell him about the rest of the things I saw, I knew how to get the truth... Watch and Wait. I had a girlfriend ride by the house when I left for work the next time and sure enough, a darn house party was taking place. He was like a teenager with vacationing parents.

Also, there was this girl from his past named Tanya who was sponsoring his daily clothing, gas and fun money. He spent time with her while I was working. I knew this because he talked in his sleep. Tanya lived close enough to his mother's house for him to leave and call me from his mom's whenever he needed an alibi. Even worse, Tanya owned his cell phone. I found that out a few hours after our wedding when she drove up and demanded it back because she'd heard of the marriage. I tossed it into her car window and she sped off.

Divorced...NOT Devastated

Once Trevor knew that I'd figured him out, I noticed that often he would start an argument with me on the way to the airport so I wouldn't want to communicate too much during my time away at work. He was so good at taking my words and using them to his advantage; making me seem like a typical angry, jealous black woman. I had to become very conscious and clever with my words. It was hard to communicate effectively during my time away.

We were in over our heads, trying to live a lifestyle we couldn't afford and we eventually got evicted. We stayed with Trevor's mother while we planned to move out of state and that's when I saw what made him so dysfunctional. On one hand, she worshiped his dirty socks (yes, she did every bit of his laundry) and he could do NO WRONG. On the other hand, she would curse him 'til dust arise" and put him out of her house in a heartbeat.

Aside from the cheating, these struggles became our norm. The drinking was out of control; I spent numerous nights taking care of and cleaning up after him. The verbal and mental abuse was constant; he made me cry at least twice a week. And whenever he couldn't win the argument or was just tired of being there, he'd pack up and leave.

When we moved to North Carolina, it only got worse. Once, we even spent 48 hours in jail; a domestic cool down is what they called it. A girl that he'd met when we were in a club TOGETHER was repeatedly calling his phone at 3:30 a.m., so I answered. She was yelling about how he promised to come pick her up. I calmly asked him to get his phone and

Divorced...NOT Devastated

tell her the truth and stop her from calling. When he pushed me away and said I was "trippin", I snapped and slapped him across the face with that phone as hard as I could. He jumped up out of the bed, picked me up by the neck and slung me across the room like a rag doll. I was able to grab his phone, run down the hall and toss it far into the dark woods across from our front door. Once he went outside to retrieve it, I slammed the door and locked it. I found out moments later that apartment doors can be kicked in with ease.

One of the neighbors called the police to complain about the noise and upon their arrival they questioned us separately and took pictures of my bloody neck and his scratched up arm and face. One of the officers asked me if he'd hit me and I said, "No". He denied me putting my hands on him too, but the evidence clearly proved differently so they took us to jail. The *State vs. The Evans* was an open case.

Because this was an outstanding case for some time, I couldn't go to work as a flight attendant because I was a flight risk! I was so ashamed. We took that time to try and mend our destructive relationship. We even had a cool down period due to the courts involuntarily separating us, even though we didn't follow their orders the whole time.

Lots of our problems came from me being the breadwinner of the home. I made all of the major decisions and paid most of the bills. I also traveled for work which Trevor somehow translated to me 'leaving whenever I felt like it'. It made him feel inferior. And I personally think that this wouldn't have been the case if he had listened to my words and

Divorced...NOT Devastated

paid attention to my adamant respect for him instead of always twisting my words and re-framing situations to contribute to his victimization when needed. He was a genius at manipulation.

He hated my job and would often allude to that fact. I used to ask him if he wanted me to quit and work somewhere near home but the status it gave us over his peers was enough for him to 'deal with it'. I would say that he missed me and wanted me home more, but the truth of the matter was, he had to take responsibility during the time I wasn't around. He had to look after the children, feed them and make sure they got to school and to their other activities and practices. He also had to come home at a decent hour and actually show up to his own job...on time.

All I wanted was balance. I made great attempts to show him that money was not the deciding factor of who the 'man of the house' should be. I wanted to be a wife. I wanted to go to work and come home to my loving family who appreciated the sacrifice I made in being away in order to sustain our cushy life. I spoiled my family with so many material items; they had everything they wanted and more. I bent over backwards for Trevor and did everything in my power to crown him my king.

Contrarily, he needed me to suffer for having the better job, the ability to purchase a car, the energy to hang out with our daughters and to do the other necessary things for our household. He was jealous of the way I didn't let too much bother me and I had a go-getter's spirit. I needed my king to join me in all the great moments in life; even at the

Divorced...NOT Devastated

expense of giving him false credit for most of "our" successes. Even with such scaffolding and support, he couldn't step into the light. It was as if he wanted me, alone, to fail. He wanted me to be miserable. He abandoned me in so many ways; He withheld sex, came home late or not at all, dissed me in front of his friends that I didn't even know, talked about me to his family and even allowed his mother to talk horribly about me and to me.

I fought for my marriage even when I saw clear ways out. We had so many ridiculous disputes and endless days of not speaking to one another. I ignored the signs from the beginning and we ended up separated for two long years.

Trevor tried to court me during our separation. He would ask for some of my time so we could have an "adult conversation." It was inconsistent and like a game to him. Although I was fed up with his shenanigans, I agreed a few times. We would start off great, then commence to telling each other how we really felt and spiral into an argument. We'd go our separate ways and try again a couple months later. The whole time, I never ignored any of his phone calls. I still wanted to be with my husband, if he could just change his ways.

In the midst of our separation, I lost my job. It was rough; I worked three jobs trying to stay afloat. The toughest part was watching him parade around like life was simple. He had new clothes, a new car, regularly vacationed and carried on while I was scraping up money to keep my lights on. He made sure to flaunt it, too. I was furious, because whenever he was down and out, I'd ALWAYS helped him. I felt like a gutted fish, but guess what?! I was still deeply in love with my husband.

He convinced me in January of 2017 to start dating him with the serious intent to work on renewing our marriage. It was amazing! We dated like never before, we laughed and spent all of our time together. I could tell he really missed me. We found our friendship and *I fell in love all over again.* We even started filming a mini YouTube show that was quickly gaining popularity. We talked about our wonderful date nights, scrutinized hot topics, told jokes and used our favorite catch phases. It was all good on camera, but most times I had to beg him to get out of bed for recording. He enjoyed the feedback from our audience but gave me such a hard time for wanting to put in the work to make it good.

Well, that all lasted for about a solid three months. Once our re-connection was established, it was astonishing how fast things shifted right back to the way they were. I couldn't fathom what was happening! I'd let my guard down! I'd opened my heart! I'd let him back in! I'd played the fool.

Let me take a moment to explain the part that ended it all. I was out driving for Uber when I had this crazy pain shooting through my torso at every angle imaginable. One of my passengers was trying to get me to answer a question and I just went totally mute. My ears were ringing and my eyes hazed over. That's when I knew something was very wrong.

Divorced...NOT Devastated

The trip back to my side of town was agonizing. It took me an eternity to get home and stumble up the stairs to my bedroom. I took two TUMS and slumped into the bed next to my resting husband. He never even acknowledged my presence, let alone tried to see why I was whimpering. A long four hours passed as I tried to 'sleep it off'. A sudden urge to urinate grabbed my attention and as I stood to walk towards the bathroom, I fell straight to the floor. My daughter came running into the room and declared that it was time to take me to the hospital. All this commotion atop of the hours of moaning and crying commenced without one single word from my husband who was right there the entire time. Nope, he didn't even go to the Emergency Room with us. As a matter of fact, he went to work. When my daughter called to tell him that I needed an emergency appendectomy, he said that he didn't want to leave the job and incur any points. Points! I was moments from death and he gave zero concern. He eventually came to the hospital, and that was enough to affirm my idiotic love for him.

The next morning he and I found out together that the CAT scan revealed a tumor consuming over eighty percent of my right kidney.

The nephrologist alerted me that it was imperative that I have the organ removed immediately. I went home with my head held high and spirit soaring because I knew that God, along with my family, would see me through this challenge!

Well, it was a good thing I had my mother and daughters around because my husband went missing. I saw him for only moments throughout the day and he may have hugged me twice over the course of the next three days. I was sad on top of afraid and lonely at night. Where was his shoulder for me to cry on, his chest for me to lie on, his arms for me to fall into? Why did he abandon me just days after this critical news? These were mere questions thought, for I was too weak to do anything about them.

With ten days until my next surgery, my mom felt herself getting ill and drove to the hospital for diagnosis and a quick remedy. She was appalled to find out that it wasn't that simple. She called me with the report and I wanted to get there and be with her as she had traveled miles from home to ensure my care and needs were met. So, I called Trevor and asked him to pick me up from home and drop me off at the hospital. He said, "Sure, I'm about fifteen minutes away."

Two and a half hours went by and he still hadn't showed up. I called and called and finally he answered, "I'm sorry Kesh, I'm on my way." Another forty-five minutes passed. He kept sending me to voicemail. Three hours into my wait he calmly called and said, "My bad (fault), I'm right down the street at the gas station, I'll be there in five minutes." I was so angry but I just said, "Okay"; I was focused on getting to the hospital to see my mother. I went downstairs and stood at the curb awaiting his arrival. Those five minutes grew to twenty-something. When he finally came, I got in the car and sat with my arms crossed and legs shaking, trying not to show my fury.

Divorced...NOT Devastated

He started picking at me, begging me to say something. I wouldn't. He was spitting all sorts of insane statements; "It's your fault your mother is sick; she shouldn't be here." "You just had surgery four days ago; you're stupid for leaving the house." "You think you can save your mom or something?" I just looked in his direction and said, "Please stop talking to me."

He pushed my head with the palm of his hand and the force made me hit the window. We weren't far so I told him to take me back home. We got to the roundabout and I stepped out once the car came to a stop. I'd left my phone on the seat so he put it on the windshield near the hood and told me to get it. As soon as I reached for it he stepped on the gas. I held on for dear life! He sped around that roundabout two times with my body flailing halfway off the car and my grip growing weaker and weaker. I was yelling as loud as I could but none of my neighbors came to my rescue. When he stopped, my body slid to the concrete and he jumped out of the car and dragged me to the passenger side and dumped me into the front seat. He said, "I came here to take you somewhere and you're going!"

I caught my breath and the tears were steadily streaming down my face, but I was silent. We were going so fast and I was afraid for my life. We came to a stop sign. I opened the door attempting to get out! I had one foot on the ground and he hit the gas. The door flung wide open with my fist still clenching the handle. He grabbed my arm and I thought he was going to pull me back in but he pushed me out even further. I managed to grab some part of the seat. I mustered up enough strength to

Divorced...NOT Devastated

pull myself back inside. I remember looking at his face, he was smiling and when we finally slowed down, he turned to me and screamed, "Close my fucking door!" We proceeded through the light and my crying must have worked his last nerve because he reached up and grabbed a handful of my hair and slammed my head down onto the middle console. I started yelling, "I'm sick, I'm sick!" He replied softly, "you're not sick" I just sat there; I didn't want to give him any more ammunition to use as an excuse to further punish me.

We pulled up to the hospital. Somehow I got brave enough to ask him where he had been for the last four days. I didn't wait for an answer, I just found myself shouting, "You don't love me, you don't care about me, I hate you!" Before I got out I grabbed the one thing that he loved, his phone. However, I made one mistake and left my own phone on the seat...again. He spotted my phone before realizing I had his and he threw it out of the window and told me to go fetch it. I held his phone up in the air and screamed at the top of my lungs "You go get it or else this is coming through your windshield!" He said, "No. You're going to pass me my phone and get the hell away from me before I kill you." I quickly gave in and followed his instructions precisely. He drove out of the parking lot and left me standing in the grass. I tried so hard to pull myself together as I picked up my phone, wiped my face, and pretended to be okay. My eyes were blood-shot red and my face was swollen, so my mother knew something was wrong the moment I pulled back the curtain in her room.

Divorced...NOT Devastated

I was just simmering down when my phone rang and it was my daughter. She was crying, explaining how Trevor had stormed into the apartment fussing and cussing and packing up his things. She said he took the television out of my room and stomped a hole in it before he left.

It was traumatizing. When my mom and I got back home, I checked in on my daughter who was upset with me for allowing Trevor back into our lives in the first place. She reluctantly gave me a hug and I headed straight to my room for prayer. I fell asleep during my talk with God, but I recall hearing Him say, "It's for your good."

Over the next week I prepared for my kidney to be removed. I also had an epiphany that ALL cancers were being removed from my body and my life, Trevor was just the first to go. I was free from the worry and different aspects of pain I had suffered as his wife. I no longer had to pretend that my marriage was working. I could live peacefully.

I filed for a divorce June 30th and it was finalized September 1, 2017.

Divorced...NOT Devastated

Lessons Learned:

I learned that God will put situations in place to reveal the truth and sometimes those situations may seem cruel and ugly.

Jealousy and competition are detrimental to any relationship. If mates can't find their position in the marriage and trust that the kingdom is well, chaos will reign.

Naturally, I'm not a yelling, screaming and cursing type of woman but early on, my coping mechanism became speaking his language. That was a disastrous choice of behavior.

The divorce was easy for me, I did not mourn, I did not shed one tear. I did that too much during the marriage. I am grateful. I am released from what bound my loving spirit and true happiness.

The above statement does not mean that I escaped unbroken. I have a lot of healing to do and when I am whole and confident in myself I will be ready to fully open my heart. It takes patience and diligence to amply access ourselves and allow the wounds and scars to mend. As they do, the genuine smiles and laughter returns and your freedom is an award you display in the fullness of life. You can LIVE!

Divorced...NOT Devastated

Questions:

1. Do you believe that a true commitment to a union is to be prepared to leave a career as a sacrifice for your mate's happiness? What if it's your family's main or only source of income?
2. If there was a scale to measure sacrifice for your mate's happiness, self esteem and security, where would you rank?
3. What sacrifices do you deem "healthy?" What sacrifices do you deem "unhealthy?" Be sure to take the time to identify both "healthy" and "unhealthy" sacrifices made in your relationships.

Angela Brown

Divorced...NOT Devastated

Angela Brown

Angela Brown attended North Carolina Central University. She has taught with the Durham County Public school system for over 12 years.

She describes herself as follows: I am a mother and a teacher. I am also divorced. My journey of married woman to single woman is one that caused me to become deeply reflective of myself. From dealing with doubt to questioning my need for societal acceptance to experiencing breakthroughs with my faith, I share with you the lessons I gleaned from my introspective probing on the quest to rediscovering myself.

Disillusionment

Tall (6'4 ¾"), dark chocolate, and handsome. Those are the words that flashed through my mind as the man with the brilliant smile crossed my path. I was at college, going back to become a teacher, and visiting my cousin that ran the Dance Department. He was in the middle of a weight workout with the football team. He told me he had to come out and talk to me. We ended up exchanging numbers. And so it began. Well, kinda.

I guess I was a little bit impressed. He was younger than I was and interested. We eventually ended up speaking on the phone several times and finally going out on a date. I don't remember the first thing we did but I remember subsequent dates. Going to get a fish sandwich from the best fish place in town. I remember going to the house where he was boarding and joking with him about having company. He didn't have any - at least that was his story. Our dates were inconsistent. Then the communication between us dwindled down and became nonexistent.

A while later we reconnected at the local library. I was there with my current friend. I ran into HIM there and we spoke for a little while. He left. And I continued browsing for books. When we got to my car, I noticed a piece of paper under my windshield wiper. I think he wrote-

Divorced...NOT Devastated

"The Future" and his phone number. I couldn't believe his audacity - but I couldn't help feeling a little pleased. It was boldness in living color. And a part of me liked that.

I was no longer with that friend. HE and I started talking again. He was full of confidence and positivity. We began to speak more consistently then. At that point he was no longer in school but out in the workforce. I had my career as a teacher. We started to communicate and date.

Our dating flowed into a relationship. I remember going on one of my favorite dates with him. We decided to go to the lake with our books and read. We literally read, with our backs to each other, on a huge rock. It was different and so relaxing. I loved it.

Dating was fun. When we got along it was perfect. I remember going to the beach with him. On one occasion, went to hear a timeshare pitch in exchange for a cruise ship vacation. We laughed on the way there and promised to not get swayed by the sales pitch - no matter how appealing. After being impressed with the company but refusing to buy a timeshare, we happily took our cruise ship vouchers and headed for the next adventure which turned out to be eating at a restaurant with tables available over the water. We flirted and joked over Caribbean and Mexican-inspired coastal seafood dishes. After our late lunch, we held hands on the boardwalk and laughed over YouTube videos. Later we drove to Beaufort to see the wild horses he heard about when he was a boy. While driving down a road in the town, we looked out the window

Divorced...NOT Devastated

and saw the horses running on the island parallel to the land. It was magical and also earned the distinction of being one of my best date experiences. Those were parts of the good times.

The bad times were also present. I remember us getting into arguments that escalated into screaming matches. It got to the point where I literally enlisted a friend to act as a mediator between the two of us so we could work on our communication issues. The endeavor was not successful. I remember feeling a certain way, but trying to hide how he hurt my feelings when we wouldn't speak for days. I thought I was showing that I wasn't jealous when I didn't comment on our silence towards on another. I remember finding an earring in his bed once. He told me that his roommate had friends over that used his bed sometimes. The earring was probably left by one of those guys having a secret rendezvous with some girl they just met. His roommate corroborated the story. It just didn't sit right in my mind… who would allow another man to use his bed like that?! An earring was left - they didn't even wash the sheets after those encounters?! We had disagreements over that subject and many more. I remember once having an argument in the car with him. I asked him to pull over and I got out of the car. I was going to walk back to his apartment, get my car, and go home. I stormed off and he drove beside me. I eventually got back into the car. I don't even remember what the argument was about.

During our relationship, we went through a lot of changes. I mentioned before that he stopped going to school. He always shared his dream of going back to school. I was fully supportive of that idea. He was

Divorced...NOT Devastated

working a job for which he felt he was overqualified. He knew that job was not what he wanted to do for the rest of his life. He shared with me that he always saw the managers of the company and knew he should be one of them. I was impressed with his ambition. He asked me what I thought of him going back to school. I was team him. "Yes, baby, I think that is a good idea." He enrolled at another college and went back to school. Two or three years later, he graduated. Throughout his years there I was super supportive. He told me he wanted to start a business with his friend while at school. I bought him business cards to help promote his business. I also bought him a fax machine to help him conduct business. I wanted to show him that I fully supported all of his dreams. I was proud of him. He was on the football team and I tried to attend all of his home games and some away games. He asked my opinion about joining a fraternity. I honestly told him I felt it would be beneficial in the workforce. I thought about my job and how so many people that worked there were part of the Greek life. He joined a fraternity. He was doing well academically. He was selected to represent his school at the Model UN. I was SO proud of him. I thought that would give him a tremendous edge on his resume *and* he would learn so much from the experience. I didn't realize I would also learn from that experience - about him and me.

I found out that while in NYC for the Model UN conference, he met another woman. One day, after using his phone, I found out that they had been communicating daily via phone, text, and social media. He had even sent her a package. Faced with the incriminating evidence, he had no choice but to admit to the truth. I broke up with him. The break up was not forever despite my gut telling me it should be so. He came back on bended knee (literally), crying how much he needed me. I caved in. We continued the relationship but I was now operating under mistrustful feelings.

He graduated from college and ended up securing a job with a company in New York City. Our relationship became long distance. He eventually moved back to NC. One day, while I was preparing food for Christmas dinner, he got on his knee and proposed with a beautiful ring. I immediately asked if he had gotten permission from my father. He said "yes," so I said "yes." We were engaged.

THE MARRIAGE

I got pregnant on the honeymoon. Yes, I am part of the small minority of women that can make that claim! I was ecstatic but not everyone shared that sentiment. Getting married and living with someone for the first time can be hard. It takes adjustments to share your life and space with another person. We were going to quickly find that truth out. He moved into my townhouse and the problems became magnified.

Pregnancy hormones and the first year of marriage definitely didn't match. I was older and my body was probably shocked by the magnificent task of creating a new life. I was extremely tired. There were times when I had just enough strength after work to drag myself to bed. My lethargy left household chores neglected. My body was working on overload. I did not have the understanding that I felt I needed from him.

Divorced...NOT Devastated

Harsh words were spoken and feelings were hurt. It seemed like we only argued. It got to a point where I suggested we attend couples counseling. He agreed.

We went to counseling. I think the doctor felt that our problems were pretty small or at least something we could get over. I guess in hindsight, the problems weren't as significant as those I see on Divorce Court, but the problems: communication, lack of empathy, selfishness, etc. were big to me/us. And they grew and grew and grew until they ballooned out of control. Distance and coldness grew between us. We slept in separate rooms. Life was not the happy ending you saw on television shows and movies.

The baby was born and our relationship continued to deteriorate. It got to the point where my stomach would literally feel like it was in knots when he was around. It was unbelievable to me that my body would react that way to my situation at the time. I was worried about being a bad example for my son. I decided to get in contact with a lawyer. We separated - and remained in that state for five years.

AFTER

It was a hard decision to leave, but ultimately I left. I weighed the pros and cons. I worried about how the split would affect my son, but I also thought about how he would be affected if we stayed in our current state. It was rough - I got on government assistance for a while and I became acquainted with the local food banks. My body was stressed and stopped producing milk during that time period. I fought feelings of failure - in both relationship and body.

My family and faith have played big roles in helping me through the dark times. I also started to go to a fabulous psychologist. I worked through my feelings. I am a better person from this experience. I am still navigating through this journey and there are a lot of things I am leaving out. However, I found the strength to leave and persevere in this new chapter in my life. I am telling this story from my perspective. I know he has a lot to say about my role in the demise of our relationship. I can only share my experience in the hopes that it can teach others on how to do better in their relationships.

LESSONS LEARNED

I never dreamt of the perfect wedding when I was younger. Some girls pick out the perfect wedding dress, hair style, location, and colors by the time they are 12. I was never that person. I just assumed that I would be married. I grew up with both of my parents and in my mind, marriage was just a natural progression in life. I had this assumption that everything would work out just because. I wish I had the foresight to focus on the important aspects of marriage – those details that are needed to help people live together forever. My reflections (still ongoing) are shared here as I think about the time I spent as someone's wife.

Divorced...NOT Devastated

1. **Independence is OVERRATED!** "I am an independent woman" is a phrase that has become popular among my generation. It is pressed upon most women as a mantra necessary for survival. "You can't depend on a man to take care of you" has been repeated so much that it is imprinted on my DNA! While those sayings are true, I feel like sometimes the message becomes too literal. Let me explain. I was already established when I got married. I had a career, car, and townhouse. I was used to taking care of myself and doing things my way. I had gotten this far on my own so it must have been something (or a lot of things) that I was doing right! Or so I thought. I wasn't thinking clearly. Once married, my husband moved into my house. You caught that? MY house. In my mind, I worked for it, had the credit to obtain it; I made the mortgage payments AND paid the HOA fees. It was MINE, not ours. And he felt that attitude. It came across in the way I addressed him, how I felt about our household bills, and probably in other ways that I am not yet cognizant of. It is important to make sure you take care of yourself, but it is equally important for both partners to be and feel needed. This concept is essential for life, period; it goes beyond marriage and touches all aspects of life. It is good to be independent but it is equally important to be interdependent.

2. **Strength.** I always admired single moms for their strength. I admired them but, in the back of my mind, I always thought it was a position in which I would never find myself because I saw

it as being too much work. Ha! The joke is on me. My alarm goes off at 4:45 am and I am literally doing something until around 10 pm. Every weekday. I am thankful that I find the strength to persevere. I found a strength inside myself that I did not know existed.

3. **Doubt/uncertainty is normal.** When I realized that staying in my marriage was not the best decision for myself and my family, doubt clouded the entire process. Don't get me wrong - doubt is important. It causes one to think fully and focus on an issue at hand. It can be used to solve the very problem that created its existence. But doubt can also become a detriment when one becomes stuck in it. I had a lot of questions revolving in my mind before I initiated the separation which would eventually lead to divorce. I wondered how would I raise my son? How would my parents feel? How would I be viewed? We weren't married long - how would that look to other people?! I didn't want to be a single parent. That is a lot of responsibility. Am I "giving up" on the marriage too soon?

One day I saw a show that was about hoarders. You know, the people that aren't able to let go of their possessions and they amass a lot of stuff that affects their home environment. It is like they almost become buried with stuff they cannot let go of. The episode I watched showed a woman that decided to stay in a marriage for the sake of her son. In one scene she was explaining

Divorced...NOT Devastated

her choice to stay in the marriage that eventually caused her to become a hoarder and the next scene showed the husband and son talking about her!! I realized that sometimes WE need to make decisions for ourselves that can initially be uncomfortable because of the fear of the unknown that end up working out in the long run. I did not want to imagine my future with me sitting in a pile of junk- figuratively or literally- because I wasn't able to let go of something that was proving to be unhealthy. I need myself more than that. My son needs me more than that. I can't imagine how that mother felt when she watched the episode with her son siding with his father as they questioned why they hadn't gotten rid of the mother earlier.

4. **Myself. Do I see myself clearly? Am I who I think I am?** I see myself as a person that is genuine, caring, open minded, and introspective. I think I get along well with others. My divorce made me reflect on myself as a person. Am I really as open minded and affable as I think I am? I am an introvert and sometimes it is hard for me to share my feelings. I have discovered the importance of projecting a true representation of yourself to others.

5. **Relationship Goals?!** We are living in the world of social media. It is a crazy place where people can cultivate any image they want to represent themselves 24/7. It is a time where a lot of people look at pictures and cute memes and tell themselves it is reality.

Divorced...NOT Devastated

Social media is the cliche "keeping up with the Jones'" on steroids! This is especially true for relationships. Let Instagram tell it, everyone is in a loving relationship that should be the envy of everyone viewing it. Viewers see Beyonce and Jay-Z and all of the sudden that couple becomes relationship goals. Awww, look at how they are staring lovingly into each other's eyes, he inspires her to write songs about their love for each other. GOALS! No one knows what is actually going on behind closed doors. We just see this perfect relationship captured in carefully selected images by professional photographers. It is astounding that people think perfection is normal. Life is not perfect - it is a series of highs and lows, disappointments and achievements. But some of us think these relationships on social media are perfect. These "relationship goal couples" don't have the photographers snapping pictures of them sitting on a therapist's sofa crying over the hurtful actions of a significant other or showing us the time it takes to rebuild trust that is broken. We see a false reality, think it applies to our real life, and get mad when the reality of relationships slaps us in the face. They are hard and take work. That should be the real hashtag.

6. **Faith.** Trust in God. Psalms 55:22 says, *Give your burdens to the Lord, and he will take care of you. He will not permit the godly to slip and fall.* A lot of time good messages are repeated so often that we actually overlook the jewel that is being presented to us. There

are plenty of events that happen to us on a daily basis that can cause us to feel overwhelmed; divorce is one of those things. I had to learn how to not worry about every single issue that came to my mind and focus on putting my trust in God. It is a work in progress because I like to be in control of my life. Sometimes things that are so easy are actually the hardest to put in practice because of our own minds. But we have a creator that wants to take care of our burdens. I just take a deep breath and remind myself that I am not alone. 1 Peter 5:10 says, *And the God of all grace, who called you to his eternal glory in Christ, after you have suffered a little while, will himself restore you and make you strong, firm, and steadfast.* This scripture gives me hope. It lets me know that I will go through rough times but God will make me strong again. I just have to be righteous. The fire (our situation) forges strength.

7. **My concept of love.** I thought everyone experienced love the way I did from my parents and family. Time and time again, I found out I was wrong. I finally figured out that love isn't words. Words are easy and cheap and can be spoken by anyone. Words can be empty. To me, love is action. It's one thing to say something, but can you do it? Action means work and that is harder because it requires more - time, effort, and, consistency. Love is DOING something you may not want to do but you are willing to for another. Love is compromise. Love is selfless. Love is rewarding. I realize I got hurt because I didn't recognize that love is action.

8. **Society's view on marriage/single mothers**. I wore my wedding ring set well into my separation. I was always cognizant of the fact that I was a young black woman with a baby. I did not want to be the stereotypical single mother with a child - or at least give that perception. I realized that I was not truly accepting of my situation as a single mother. In fact, it dawned on me that I was totally misrepresenting myself to the public. What is it about society that caused me to feel that way? No, what is it about myself that caused me to feel that way? I had to grow to the place where it doesn't matter what anyone else thinks about me.

9. **Support in numbers**. We cannot live this life successfully alone. Even our bodies were made to complement each other (think our genitalia). We fit together. I have mentioned that I am an introvert. I can be completely satisfied with being by myself for days on end. I am not bored with my own company! At some times, I rather enjoy it. However, that isn't always healthy. We need one another to survive. That truth has not been clearer to me as a single mother. I am not able to do everything on my own. I may get sick and need help. I may need advice on a specific issue I am facing with my son. It is always great to hear multiple perspectives. My family has provided much needed support in this process of divorce and raising a child. There is a popular phrase "it takes a village to raise a child." That is so true. We are not able to do everything alone. It is ok to need and accept help. There is a myth that black women are strong and we can take

Divorced...NOT Devastated

care of everything. That is not true. We were not meant to be one-woman armies. I am raising my son with the support of an entire village surrounding us. Support in numbers is not confined to child rearing. Joining the DND collaborative has given me strength as an individual too. It is comforting to know that there are other women going through similar situations. It is comforting to know there are success stories. It is comforting to know that I am not an island - that other women have experienced the same feelings and we are overcoming difficulties together! Black women as a group are the most educated group of people. I think it is because we see each other and know that we are capable of more. If my sister can do it, then I can too! It isn't about pride or jealous, it is about support. It is a winning mindset that can be applied to everything. Support is necessary.

Divorce does not mean devastation. For me, marriage and then divorce created a situation that became a field of personal growth. I have learned a lot from this process; from the way I view myself, to the way I process and learn from changes, to even strengthening my relationship with God. I am reaping the benefits and continuing to learn/grow more. I hope this reflection is able to help you in the way you view yourself and your relationships. Experience + Strength = Growth

Author Janera Harvey

Janera Harvey

Janera Harvey, MPH, is a daughter, mother, author, entrepreneur, and a behavioral health manager for a behavioral health company. She has a diversified background in the medical industry that spans from pre-respiratory therapy training to pharmaceutical sales. Throughout the years, she has been active within the community by partnering with non-profit organizations to assist with providing health education to minority women and mentoring young women in the community. A lady who has a heart for people, Janera also organized a women's ministry, "G.W.I.N: God's Women in Network", which she started in her home and expanded to her former church. This ministry was a platform where women from all walks of life came together to uplift, motivate, pray, serve, and offer support.

Recently, she started a business that focuses on real estate investing. While operating her business, Janera stays committed to her three sons, works for a company that focuses on saving the lives of those who struggle with substance abuse, and actively serves in her church and community. Aside from her active schedule, she can be found enjoying family and friends via social events and travel.

Enough

In the late 80's a movie titled, "Baby Boom" came out. Diane Keaton portrayed the lead character; whose name was J.C. Wiatt. Here I was, this young brown girl, yet I connected with this character. I saw this woman of power; she commanded respect and held her own in both the board room and her personal life. J.C was married to her high- profile job and addicted to success. Her focus never wavered; she was known by those in her professional circle as – *the tiger lady*. She did manage to have a superficial relationship with Steven, an investment broker; but her job was always top priority.

Most girls, when growing up, dreamed of Prince Charming coming into their lives and taking them to a place called "Happily Ever After". My mother has always told me, for as far back as my memory takes me, "be just as unique as your name, I named you *Janera* for a reason". I must say, as a young girl I dreamed differently, and Prince Charming wasn't in existence when I envisioned my future life.

I was 20 years old; an acquaintance contacted me, and he said he just wanted to go out and have fun. I agreed. We went out and it was fun; nothing serious. We found ourselves hanging out often; almost like a couple. I was trying to avoid this, since I was still grieving from a previous relationship. Hanging out with this guy enabled me not to think about a lost love, but actually forced me to start living again. Months passed, and things just evolved; suddenly, the friendship transitioned into sexual intimacy. Then, the sexual intimacy kept happening and I became pregnant... this was NOT part of my J.C. Wiatt plan.

How could this happen to me?! You see, I told myself that I would not have any kids any time soon, and not out of wedlock. The timing was off, and I could barely take care of myself, let alone a baby. I was afraid... how could I tell family and this man that I was pregnant? What would people think? What would my friends think? I knew I was not ready for children. He knew that I loved God and that I couldn't grieve God by getting rid of the child. The truth was, I didn't want to have a baby with him. He was nice and fine, but in my eyes he wasn't who I would choose for a husband. The thought about not keeping this man's child entered my mind. This man embraced me, he told me that I had nothing to worry about and that I should keep the child and that we would make it work. Even as he said "trust me" I doubted his word. He told me that he was a good dad and that he would take care of me and the child, just like he took care of his current child. Well, I witnessed him taking care of his child and I said "okay." Here's what I didn't know; this was his way to trap me.

Here I am pregnant, determined not to have a baby out of wedlock and to not be on welfare.... I said yes to being married. I knew that this was not the time for me; there were so many signs! However, my fears of what others would say about my circumstances led me to the alter.

Determined to be grown and too prideful to go home, my life had changed overnight and it was depressing. Blinded by my false sense of security, I walked naively into a union with a struggling alcoholic who had major issues with self-control and every form of abuse. Instead of the blissful union that I was now willing to settle for, I found myself forced to fight for my own survival within my home!

How could I not know these things? Was I that caught up in the situation that I was blinded by everything else that was going on around me? Did I just choose to not see the signs and let my vision of how marriage should be motivate me, instead of looking at my reality? I was raised in a home where I saw no arguing, nor fighting. I knew how to defend myself if I was being picked on outside of the house, but I didn't know how to fight inside my home. This was my husband; I was supposed to be his cheerleader, not his punching bag. I took the first kick to my stomach while I was pregnant. My drunk husband kicked me and our unborn child because I was on the phone talking to my hometown pastor and my husband assumed I was cheating. My voice within was crying for me and my child, fearing my baby would be damaged. The cramps were like contractions and I knew this was gonna turn out bad. The baby was alright but this was the beginning of my marital turmoil.

As years progressed, more babies came. Dysfunction was the new normal; it took many run ins with the law, DUI's, probation and then

Divorced...NOT Devastated

the courts appointing him to a treatment facility before things got right. As the fights subsided and things became somewhat peaceful, we started a business. With issues such as my husband's alcoholism still not in check and plaguing our household, it was difficult to find balance. As we prepared to repair the family and grow the business, my health started to take a turn for the worse. The countless stresses first caused me to have Bell's Palsy. I looked like I'd had a stroke. I was drooling, had slurred speech, and couldn't close my eyes; I could barely eat. I hated this! I felt so ugly and I didn't want to socialize with anyone. Why was this happening to me?! I would say this so much that it was my new language.

After overcoming the Bell's Palsy, my health took a turn for the worse again. I kept having these stomach pains, I stayed in the bathroom with constant vomiting and diarrhea, even though I hadn't eaten anything. I kept begging my husband for help, but he wouldn't help me. Our second born was at the bathroom door crying for me but I couldn't get to him. Lying on the sofa, my husband said, I need "to stop faking and get the baby" while he lay on the sofa.

Although the physical abuse had died, the emotional abuse was alive and thriving. Luckily I had the phone in the bathroom and I called my mom telling her about my vomiting and diarrhea. She asked me if it was black and looked like coffee grounds and I said yes. My mother told me that was blood and I needed to get to the hospital. As she was telling me this, she could hear my husband yelling in the background, telling me to "hurry up and get out the bathroom and shut our baby up." He

Divorced...NOT Devastated

wouldn't call for an ambulance so I had to drive myself because he said he wouldn't spend that money on me faking.

By the grace of God I made it to the ER and they confirmed that I was bleeding and I was put on medicine for ulcers. Once this was controlled by my physician, a new issue came. I started missing my menstrual cycles and this went on for a year. Every month I had to take a pregnancy test. My doctors would run tests and there was nothing. Once again, it was attributed to marital stress. My body didn't know how to do the things that it does naturally; it just stopped. Once again I began questioning God and his plan for my life.

My doctor put me on medication to regulate my cycle. It worked. I was so happy to feel normal again. I was mentally planning my escape; how I would get out of the environment and live happy; maybe even go back to school and finally get my bachelors degree. I started researching schools, planning to go online so that I could be home with my babies. I was creating a plan and it was going to be without a husband. I narrowed my selection down to two colleges. Once I did this, I told my husband that I wanted to finish my degree and go back to school. We could afford it, the business was growing and I didn't have to work. I was sure my husband would support me after all the years of supporting him through recovery, him going back to school and helping him develop the business that we had. My husband told me that I couldn't go back to school. I needed support and growth. I became the rebellious wife and pursued anyway.....I had a plan. I didn't care anymore, ENOUGH!!! Then unthinkable happened, my cycle didn't come again. What in the world,

Divorced...NOT Devastated

more health issues. I just can't get a break, right when I was starting to feel alive again. I went to my doctor and they gave me a pregnancy test. POSITIVE, I was pregnant!!!

During the first trimester of the pregnancy, I immediately started to have problems. One day, I went to the bathroom and started passing clots. It was like a menstrual cycle on steroids; the clots wouldn't stop. Immediately, I knew I was losing the baby. This was a fear of unknown for me; my baby was in the toilet is all I could think and why was this happening. I immediately went to the doctor and was told that I was having a miscarriage. I was devastated. I never experienced loss like this and my husband didn't even comfort me. I requested labs be drawn for me to believe that this was happening to me. The blood work would show that my hormone levels are decreasing but in actuality, my levels had gone up. The doctor and the nurses said this was impossible, so they had me get an emergency ultrasound.

There I was alone at the Imaging Center, waiting to get my ultrasound. No baby appeared on the monitor. I had no support; I was scared. This was our child and he wasn't there. A week later additional labs were ordered and my hormone levels were much higher than before. Here I was again, confident knowing my baby was in place. My doctor did another ultrasound...no baby. Now I'm an emotional wreck and all kind of fear was growing inside of me; what was going on? Another ultrasound was ordered, this time the tech put the ultrasound gel below my abdomen and began to scan as far down as she could...no baby. My doctor was contacted because now I was getting my ultrasounds done at the hospital. He said, "Do a vaginal ultrasound"....ugh!!!

A heartbeat.......there was my baby! A huge gasp came out of my mouth; I just knew my baby was there. Unfortunately, those clots were his twin and the baby that was holding on was so far down in the vaginal canal, the doctors weren't sure he would make it. Now, I was considered a high risk pregnancy and had to get ultrasounds every week until my due date, to monitor the baby and myself closely. Luckily, both of us were just fine and I delivered successfully. After the birth of my "Miracle Baby," I started having more menstrual complications. This time things were really bad and led to a hysterectomy at the age of 28.

The marriage had a new devil and things started spiraling out of control. From one addiction to another...gambling. This may not seem big to many but it was in my house. Bills were going unpaid, money was missing that we had in the house and in the banks. Tenants started to come to our house saying that there was a foreclosure notice placed on their door. How could the man of the house allow this to happen? I'd question him and the response given was that he'd take care of it. In my mind, I was thinking that he wasn't taking care of it which is why we were starting to have these problems. Now, not only was I faced with this new devil but his old devil reemerged as well. Before I knew it, I had to start fighting in my house again. He didn't make me feel safe in any area of our marriage; I couldn't stay and I needed to find a *way out quick*!

Divorced...NOT Devastated

We had an argument one night; it got heated...really heated. All I remember him saying is I'll kill you and take the boys. He grabbed me from behind and put my head in a way that I couldn't breathe. It was like a wrestling move, he took my head and snatched it in a way to make my neck pop. Nothing but God kept me that night. I got away and called my parents crying and in pain. He threw me and the babies out of our home. Envision Tyler Perry's movie "The Diary of a Mad Black Woman" when the character was thrown out of her home. It was cold and I sat on my lawn with my babies until my parents drove almost an hour to get us.

You see, so many times we allow fear to hold us back. Unknowingly, we placed ourselves in a prison called bondage. There was the fear of the unknown, the fear of "I don't know how", the fear of walking away from the life I knew and starting all over with three babies. I had ENOUGH and finally stepped out on faith.

After finally leaving my husband of nine years (ten years together) I had to learn how to live and function as a single mom. My ex-husband pretty much took care of the financial responsibilities of the home while I worked and maintained the house and parented our children. Life was getting ready to teach me how to love myself again and how to raise three black boys into strong, respectable men.

I made a vow to focus the next several years on completing my education and creating a better life for me and my children. By doing this, I knew I had to make changes for myself in order to achieve in this new life. I vowed not to date and or get close to any male while I continued to

Divorced...NOT Devastated

focus on my studies. I committed to working extra hard during the weekends that my boys were visiting their dad. I worked at a medical office and many times when the pharmaceutical reps would provide lunch, I'd bring the leftovers home for me and the boys. If there was only enough for the boys, then that's how our night would end up.

Psalm 23 (NIV) is what carried me through my dark days:

1 The Lord is my shepherd; I shall not want.
2 He maketh me to lie down in green pastures: he leadeth me beside the still waters.
3 He restoreth my soul: he leadeth me in the paths of righteousness for his name's sake.
4 Yea, though I walk through the valley of the shadow of death, I will fear no evil: for thou art with me; thy rod and thy staff they comfort me.
5 Thou preparest a table before me in the presence of mine enemies: thou anointest my head with oil; my cup runneth over.
6 Surely goodness and mercy shall follow me all the days of my life: and I will dwell in the house of the Lord for ever.

This is my go-to scripture; its everything that represents my life and how God walked with me. My strength comes from this scripture, my fears go away and I become emboldened when I read it. My future comes from this scripture, my faith in who God is to me comes from this scripture, my success comes from this scripture, I AM this scripture.

Divorced...NOT Devastated

What I had envisioned, became my reality. Finally, the Winter of 2005 I graduated from college with a BA degree. With God, I did it!! The presence of my beautiful sons kept me motivated. I can't describe the sense of accomplishment that I felt. I instantly wanted to do more.

I set my eyes on becoming a pharmaceutical sales rep, I had no experience, but I was determined to try. I shadowed a rep a few times not knowing that it would be a great deal of help for me later on when it came time for my interview. I felt like "The Tiger Lady" again! Thank God for the networking; I interviewed with my first pharmaceutical company and was hired.

Here I was a pharmaceutical sales rep, very far from my previous world. Just months ago I was the one telling pharmaceutical sales reps if the doctor was able to see them. I was the one who was so glad when pharmaceutical sales reps brought lunch because I used the leftover food that they provided to take home and feed my children; who would've known. Life was starting to turn around for me and my sons but things were still challenging. I was still having to face the residue from my marriage. My credit score was not where it used to be. It was hard to really enjoy the new income because I was using it to clean up the financial mess from the marriage. I was happy though. The boys were happy and we finally moved out of the cramped two bedroom apartment. I was back in school and this time I was working on my Master's degree in Public Health. My life had a new outlook and I was determined that this was just the beginning of my success. I worked hard and studied even harder. So many people doubted my successes. I was even told on

Divorced…NOT Devastated

multiple occasions that I'd never be able to complete my Master's degree with three sons and working in Corporate America with a high demanding job. I graduated with my Masters in Public Health in spite of the naysayers and obstacles.

Things really turned around for me and my sons; I was truly walking in a higher level of peace. I needed this peace because as I progressed to new levels, new devils came along with them. By this time, we had left the area, built a new home and we were good. Just because we were in a good place and walking in a new level of peace does not mean that we're exempt from the challenges that life brings forth. I will say that my journey has equipped me to handle things much better than I did during my younger years.

As I reflected, I realized that I didn't understand what that marriage would prepare me for and today I understand it. First, that marriage brought forth new standards that I had to establish that only life could teach me. I'm so grateful for every second of pain, agony and health issues that I endured during those times because I now know what to say "NO" to and I know what I don't want and need in my life that will interrupt my peace. My peace is precious.

People always ask me how I do it; raise three boys on my own, overcome great trials and still smile everyday. The answer is simple, FORGIVENESS. It's more freeing than anyone can imagine. Love you first, versus someone else. It's divine order!! Establish a relationship with God…… My walk in the valley of the shadow of death (literally); was not

Divorced...NOT Devastated

for me. I now understand that God trusted me in the valley so that I can live the rest of my life as an example of what the mountain side looks like without the devastation. My favorite response to how I do it, is Mary Mary's song "Walking."

Whatever you face, keep Walking!

Divorced...NOT Devastated

Walking

By Mary Mary

Tell me what you see when I pass by
Shadow a cloud or a light in the sky
Am I getting it wrong or am I getting it right
Well all I can take is one, one step at the time

Look at me I'm trying
Every day I fall down
Make mistakes, get back up
Try again, next time that, see me
I'm walking I'm walking I'm walking
(repeat)

Some people say walking takes too long
But I say with waking you can't go wrong, no
Why should you rush your way through life?
You won't get very far running all the time

Look at me I'm trying
Every day I fall down
Make mistakes, get back up
Try again, next time that, see me
I'm walking I'm walking I'm walking

Divorced...NOT Devastated

(repeat)

What does life say about me
Can anyone see
Does it show I rock with the greatest?
I can't get back the time I spent
Use the rest of it to show all the world how I made it

I put one foot in front of another, yes I do, yeah
And I keep on
I'm taking one day at a time
And I am steady walking
Yeah 'cause I know that Jesus walks with me
Yes he does, said I know that Jesus walks with me, yeah
So I keep on , yeah, yeah
Said I keep on walking, walking
Said I am walking, yeah

Author Ayanna Smith

Ayanna Smith

Ayanna M. Smith is a financial professional based in the Hampton Roads, Virginia area. Ayanna is a rising leader in the financial industry known for helping people grow and save money by teaching practical financial principles and concepts.

Ayanna also served America's students in the Virginia Public Education System as an elementary School Teacher & Assistant Principal for over 20 years. Ayanna's also a classically trained vocalist and is a professional singer, songwriter, and national recording artist. She's sung across the United States with well-known artists in the music industry. She's also known as a great orator, storyteller, and presenter who weaves a message of inspiration, humor and empowerment for all people. She believes that success carries a duty and obligation to impact, grow and empower the lives of others.

The Detox Is Real

I would have killed him if I could have gotten away with it. The pain, the hurt, the shame, the guilt. The embarrassment, the heartache, the sickness. I deeply experienced each of these emotions and so much more. I was on an emotional roller coaster; one that was filled with so many twists and turns. It felt as if it would never let me off. I wondered why me? How could he do this to me? What was wrong with me? Was I that bad? Did I not do enough? Did I not give enough? Did I not encourage him enough? Weren't we supposed to grow old together? What was the real problem? There were so many thoughts running through my mind and the thoughts were overwhelming and depressing. I was disappointed that I had not seen that things were unsettled and that there were changes in our relationship. We were Christians and both of us were actively involved in church ministries. We were Preachers for God's sake and this wasn't supposed to be happening. Brief side note, being a preacher does NOT exempt anyone from experiencing the ups and downs of life! We confessed to being saved and were in leadership roles, influencing others. People looked up to us. We had witnessed other peoples' relationships being attacked and broken apart and we were working together in our marriage to beat the odds. We prayed for others who were in relationships that had been

Divorced…NOT Devastated

attacked and observed that they were dog paddling and still treading water. There was hope for the survival of those marriages. With all that we believed about the sanctity of marriage, I was in disbelief that we had arrived at this point. I questioned that we have gone from being decently happy to flatline communication and I had not been aware of the decent. The silence was deafening long before I realized my hearing was impaired. We couldn't hear *relationally* anymore. So, what was I to do?

Let's go back to the beginning. It all began in college around 1994, when we were introduced to each other through mutual friends. One of my friends was the girlfriend of his best friend. We all met at the guys' apartment and engaged in general conversation. Interest was sparked. As time passed, and more time was spent together, our relationship developed, and we became an *item*. For a time, we functioned in a long-distance relationship because I'd moved out of state to take on my first professional teaching position in the Hampton Roads/Tidewater area of Virginia. That long-distance, pre-marital phase of our relationship proved to be challenging. He was upset that I was leaving. He asked, what would make me stay in Durham, NC as opposed to moving to Virginia? I responded that if we would get married I'd stay. He said that he wasn't ready for marriage. Nor, was he interested, at the time, in relocating to Virginia to secure a stable job. So, for me, the decision was a no-brainer. I was off to do what I'd obtained a college degree to do, and that was to teach children. That scenario was a red-flag, but I couldn't see it as such. The truth be told, he wasn't ready to be married and neither was I! I'd left that conversation with a made-up mind that we were over

Divorced...NOT Devastated

and done. We really weren't ready. Neither one of us had a clue of the importance of self-knowledge, self-worth, and self-esteem. We didn't realize the major impact these concepts have on one's individual development; even more so, holding implications for developing as a couple and staying together in a marriage. I will say this, marriage is not for pansies, weaklings or whiners. The full armor is required to endure the hard times as well as the good times. There is no set formula for "making it work". And, truthfully, based on some of the models of the marriages I'd observed, I am convinced that most of the couples were "flying blind."

Despite the decision to go our separate ways, he still agreed to help me move to Virginia. Emotions were strained, we weren't really talking, and he was treating me in a very cruel manner. He'd planned to get me moved into my apartment and not see me anymore. And, I was totally alright with it. I think his best friend, who'd assisted with the move to Virginia, convinced him to apologize and make up with me. And, being the soft-hearted and gullible person I was, especially when it came to him, I accepted his apology and agreed to stay in the now, long-distance relationship; over time, accruing hundreds of dollars in phone bill charges and travel costs! Wow, the things we do for what we THINK is love. A period of about two years passed as we continued our long-distance relationship. We'd alternate traveling on weekends to and from Virginia and North Carolina. We were in love and were committed to each other. We were going to make it!!! In his plans to visit me one weekend, he asked about finding a photographer because he wanted to take pictures on the

Divorced...NOT Devastated

beach. Arrangements were made with a professional photographer and during that photo shoot he proposed. I was excited and ready to plan a wedding. I was going to be a Mrs.!

We got married July 4, 1998! Right, on Independence Day! Some people made the statement that I was losing my independence. I scoffed at them for being negative. However, as the years moved on, to a major degree, I unfortunately did lose my independence. Like any couple, we experienced good times and hard financial times. There were births of nieces and nephews, deaths of loved ones, personal graduations from college, career advancement, job changes, new churches, and new friends. We went through surgeries and although undeclared, I am convinced that we also experienced a miscarriage. We went through it all together. So how in the world did we end up at this terrible place called divorce? We were supposed to make it last forever and ever! The bible says that a bill of divorcement was permitted because of the hardness of men's (and women's) hearts. I saw that in living color. The man I thought I knew, no longer existed. Without receiving the memo that he'd left the building, I had to pick up the pieces and run or end up with a federal charge or dead!

As I reflect, I believe it all started when I went to graduate school to work on my doctoral studies. This is when the changes in our relationship dynamics became noticeable; if one was looking with opened eyes. This was around the start of the seventh year of our marriage. I had completed a master's degree and now I was trying to pursue another degree on the doctoral level. I believed that getting this advanced degree would assist me in career advancement. I was optimistic that with

Divorced...NOT Devastated

achievement of this doctorate degree, I would be able to bring more revenue into our household. Moreover, with new skills, I would be more efficient and effective in my capacity as a school administrator as well as enhance and support my husband in his role as a leader in the church. Yes, I thought we were doing the Lord's work. Although we were doing a good work, all good work is not God's work.

As I was going back to graduate school to improve myself, my husband decided that he wanted to advance his role as the man and head of the household. So, he decided to move to the second shift on his job. Working on the second shift would allow him to bring more money into the home, as well as take on the leadership role. That seemed like a great plan. But, sadly, money wasn't all we needed. We were at a crossroad. The seven-year itch needed to be scratched! We needed to go back to the basics and to look at the relationship skills that had held us together to this point in our marriage. We needed to recommit to continue to grow closer. We needed to have returned to our first love, Jesus. So fast forward, I'm in graduate school, serving as an elementary school assistant principal and he's working the second shift at a reputable car insurance company in corporate America. He's getting home late and I'm up working on class assignments and sometimes talking on the phone with colleagues in the graduate program to collaborate and seek clarity. I must admit, I got comfortable doing my own thing while at home alone. I'd been used to us being home together in the evenings, but when that changed, I was lonely and found solace by talking on the phone with close friends or family. When my ex-husband would come home, I'd be in no

Divorced...NOT Devastated

rush to get off the phone because I'd gotten comfortable. Sadly, I didn't see the need to jump of the phone into the arms of my husband and share *exclusive* time with him. We'd speak and quickly share a kiss, but I now know that wasn't enough to sustain a marriage. The relationship was starving from lack of intimacy and affection. Moreover, my husband didn't share his disappointment or needs with me. The lack of communication was horrible. He expected me to just know; just read his mind and pull it all together by myself. Communication is a two-way street and both parties must candidly share in an open and honest manner; with the willingness to grow from the downfall, and redirect to make a positive change. That's the only way any relationship will even have a fighting chance of working. During this challenging time, I just milled around entertaining myself and helping my husband on the second and fourth weekends of the month, in ministry at his father's church in eastern North Carolina, From this experience, I totally know that maintaining communication is key for my future relationships. But, the lack thereof, produced fissures and cracks in our marriage that led to extra-marital affairs. The reality of the extra-marital affairs was revealed to me in a dream. I tried not to believe it, but I had to. When I confronted my husband and asked, he confirmed that it had happened. Instead of talking things out and sharing his displeasure with me, he shared that he would just go to the bedroom, turn on the television and sometimes cry himself to sleep. And, ultimately my husband had sought attention from the place where he spent most of his hours; the workplace.

Divorced...NOT Devastated

Now, I take into consideration that he was sadden by the mutual lack of communication. However, there were many situations when I shared my displeasure and disdain, but my cries and pleas went unaddressed or unheard. I'm very loyal. Security and loyalty are very important to me. However, these two areas had been challenged and broken down over time and my respect level towards my husband started to fray. My voice was slowly taken away until I didn't have one. Without really noticing, I had made him my God and I did whatever I had to do to keep the peace. Please don't misunderstand any of this. We didn't fuss or fight, verbally of physically. We had a *silence* killer. The killer that didn't talk, hear or listen.

So as the last months of our ten-and-a-half-year marriage, a total of fourteen years together, came colliding to a crashing halt, we agreed to go on a trip to Myrtle Beach with his family. I set it up and made the necessary arrangements with his family and shared the details. We traveled to South Carolina to have a good time. We'd spent most of our years of marriage working in the marketplace and in church. We'd not lived as a healthy young vibrant couple should. We spent a great deal of time trying to please others and live as we thought they would approve. What was so interesting is that the only two people paying bulls and living at our home were us. We shouldn't have given a care about any outsider's thoughts; family or otherwise. We should have been living a bondage- free life. The major devastation for me was that he and I were ministers of the Gospel. Wasn't that enough to keep us together? Apparently not, it takes more

Divorced...NOT Devastated

than lip service; it takes a life of commitment and heart service. A committed, respectful and loyal heart is golden to a relationship.

I know that I gave it all that I had in the fight for my marriage. But one thing I know; a boxer can't fight alone. An opponent is needed to declare a winner. I was fighting alone. He'd given up and wanted me to do the same. He even asked me at one point, "Why do you fight so hard?" That was one of the cues to let him go. I had to, because I was breaking down daily. I was losing myself and I was afraid that I wasn't going to come back if I kept going on these mentally unstable trips due to the infidelity and his cold heart.

Though this process I learned to regain my voice. I went to counseling immediately after learning of his infidelity. I continued personal counseling for several years thereafter. I had the support of my mother, father, sister, my maternal grandmother, and some close friends who I could use as real sounding boards; curse words and all. I had to detox; take a great big spiritual enema to flush out all the pain, hurt, guilt and shame. I took baby steps. I often felt as if I was going to die. Those who were my support system, saw me at my worst and I'm very thankful they have been able to see me transition out of that time of darkness. These people who loved me, experienced the anger and sadness right along with me. They saw me forced to leave the home my husband and I were purchasing because I couldn't afford it alone. They saw me sell off my home furnishings. They also, saw me struggle and work my way back to create a new life for myself. I know that my family was hurt in their own way due to the relationship my husband had developed with each of

Divorced...NOT Devastated

them. I can personally attest to the level of love my family had for me because my grandmother gave her life's savings to my husband, on my behalf, to start a business. That was love. So yes, my family was devastated too; they were hit in their hearts by the divorce. I'm thankful that they pushed through their personal losses and were there to support me in pushing through my losses. We have healed together and grown closer, as a result.

Has it been easy? No. Has it been stressful at times? Yes. Has it been a lonely road at times? Yes. Have the thoughts of feeling low and worthless been part of the process? Yes. Has a new voice been discovered? Yes. Has God's grace been a sustainer? Most assuredly!

As a catharsis to my pain, hurt and healing, my gift of writing poetry turned into songwriting. I was able to pen two songs, "My Friend" and "So Free" that have been a vehicle to assisting others in their fight for their freedom. I began to record in the studio. This was something that I had always wanted to do, but my ex-husband never supported me in doing so. This was a part of my internal and mental detox. Writing and recording helped me to regain my voice. I was becoming free from that controlling spirit that I had unknowingly lived under for so many years. I liken the manipulation and control to that of a boa constrictor. When a boa constrictor wraps around its prey, it does so ever so slowly. Then it slowly tightens up on the prey without them realizing it and then the prey's dead. Toxic relationships, unidentified, will produce the same effect. I was slowly dying and wouldn't have ever tried to get out. I would have died unfulfilled and settling for the mundane. Even worst, I could have ended up in prison or dead! Our marriage was headed to a dangerous place, but I give all praise to Jesus for the road to recovery and sanity. My faith, family and friends kept me alive!

God gave me these words and melodies. I sang "My Friend" into a voice recorder with tears running down my face. I was wondering what I was going to do without my husband. How was I going to make it through? I was so sad, and with a depression-filled heart the words began to flow. Meditate on the excerpts of each song and stay encouraged:

My Friend: *No one else can dry my tears and no one else can calm my fears. Oh Lord you've been my friend, Oh Lord, You have been with me until the end!*

So Free: *So free, so free and I know who I am, and I know just where I've been There wasn't a time I didn't need the Lord and His grace toward me There were so many times I didn't know what to do. If it wasn't for His love I wouldn't have made it through.*

The devastation strengthened and restored me. The gift of songwriting and singing freely had been locked away for so many years. After a decade and a half, it was time to be released. And ironically, at the penning of this chapter, ten years have passed since the divorce decree was granted in 2008. Some theorists say that the number ten is a "completeness in divine order" as well as a "completed course of time." With that, my expectations for the next decades or years of ten, are to progress to fulfill my God-given assignment as near perfect as I possibly can.

Divorced…NOT Devastated

Author Joan Sharpe McCullough

Joan Sharpe McCullough

Joan Sharpe McCullough is a Public School Administrator in Southeastern Virginia. Joan boasts many years of basketball coaching on both the high school and college levels. She is a native of Hertford County, North Carolina and a graduate of Elizabeth City State University, where she became a member of Delta Sigma Theta Sorority, Inc.

Ms. McCullough is the mother of one beautiful daughter, Brianna and family and friend to many. In her spare time, she is a blogger, podcaster, photographer, graphic designer, and an internet radio station owner (BJS Radio). Talented does not begin to describe this woman, who is largely self-taught. DND will be her literary debut, however watch out for much more to come.

The Signs Were There

As the Southern Baptist saying goes, "Trouble don't last always." Apparently, neither do long distance relationships among African-American college students. Quincy, the 6-4, 240-pound linebacker I had so confidently acquired during my junior year, had grown weary of the five-hour stretch of roadway between us and abruptly ended our relationship two years later. He had become distant and we communicated less and less until he ultimately stopped taking my phone calls.

I cried for what felt like weeks, but it wasn't until much later that I accepted the reality that most of those tears were about the rejection. I never felt secure during that relationship because I wasn't what I thought Quincy really wanted. He was the type of guy who loved women: prissy, sexy, beautiful goddesses. I was a college basketball player and a member of a Greek-letter sorority, but you'd be hard pressed to catch me in a pair of hot pants and heels.

My friends practically put me on suicide watch and took shifts with me at the local bar to keep me focused and engaged. One particular

Divorced...NOT Devastated

childhood girlfriend and I began to hangout frequently. Her brother Marcus, although three years older than us, had finally decided that we were cool enough to be seen publicly with him.

"See, he's crazy!" He said one night. Instantly I perked up, in desperate need of affirmation. "If it was me, I would have not done this to you. I would have had you AND the other girl, and you wouldn't have even known!" Pause. Drink. Wait. What?

He was so sincere, and I was so dumb. I forgave myself for the ignorance eventually because when a little girl's biological father knows she exists, yet fails to acknowledge her, or for that matter, admit that she belongs to him, how can a woman *know* innately what to accept from a man?

What's worse, the one person who always loved me unconditionally – my mother- passed away when I was only ten years old. I had extended family who raised me and made sure I was well educated and polished. However, emotionally, I was nothing but a bundle of scar tissue.

As time passed, those drinks ushered us into the bedroom where we easily confused lust, like, and love. We agreed to keep it on the low and I made it perfectly clear that I wasn't ready for a serious relationship.

When I realized that his feelings were much deeper than mine were, I immediately cut off the sexual part of the relationship and put him back into the *friend* zone. His personality changed drastically when he was

Divorced...NOT Devastated

drinking, but I figured we were just having fun. Before I knew it, Marcus was telling me exactly what my inner child needed to hear.

"I don't know why you love that red boy so much. He doesn't love you. He doesn't give a shit about you, but I'm here! Sooner or later you'll realize that I'm the man for you."

So, by the following April, I accepted the reality that the so-called love of my life was gone forever, and I gave in to Marcus's desires for a full relationship. I traded in my preferences for physique, height, and charm and accepted the shorter frame, stout stature, and foul mouth that would shame a sailor. He was nothing like Quincy, but he was there.

One evening after practice, I came home expecting to relax and unwind a bit. I grabbed a beer from the fridge and sat down on the couch beside Marcus. Almost immediately, he stormed into the kitchen and started cleaning and clanging pots and pans preparing to cook. All the while, he gave me the silent treatment. This was the first time I had experienced anything like this and I lost it. I cried hysterically trying to figure out what was going on. I kept asking him, "What's wrong with you? Why are you acting like this?" He glared at me and said, "You don't do shit! I don't even live here but I have to come over here and cook and clean!" Startled, I stood silently, unable to gather my senses. "I'm sorry" was all I could muster.

Thus, the pattern was established: perform, belittle, degrade, ignore, and then I apologize. From there, I stopped thinking of things I

Divorced...NOT Devastated

could do to make him happy and did all I could do not to make him *unhappy*. The consequences were too dire to bear.

By November, I was in depression, but had no clue why. Yes, you are reading this correctly. I really had no idea that I was in a toxic and abusive situation. Still, I had a good career, was living on my own, and was the head coach of my former high school basketball team. Who could ask for a better life?

I was on an emotional and psychological collision course trying to find myself and I was essentially empty inside. I shared everything with Marcus about my childhood, which eventually came back to bite me.

One day he responded, "Joan, did your mother ever do *anything* wrong? You act like your grandmother was the devil and your mother was a saint." My heart ached. In my memories of my mother, she *was* a saint and those memories were very precious to me. Time passed, and I sank deeper into the abyss. Barely able to get out of bed and wishing sudden death upon myself, just before Thanksgiving I made an appointment to see a psychologist. This was the first time I had ever heard these words: "Ms. Sharpe, you are clinically depressed."

I soon began therapy and got a prescription for an antidepressant. Still oblivious to my present situation, I was glad to be able to blame my past for my pain. So, I picked myself up, bought a used car in mid-December, and Marcus proposed to me at his mother's house, in front of

Divorced...NOT Devastated

his family on Christmas Eve. Caught completely off guard, I said yes. Pause. Drink. Wait. What?

The relationship was a complete train wreck with multiple casualties from the start, but I figured that I had better grab the opportunity while it presented itself. *No one else will want me with so much baggage* I thought. If this man loved me unconditionally and cherished me, then I would have been a fool to turn him down. *Finally*, I would have the love that I needed so desperately! I can say I loved him, but I hadn't been loving him long enough to be considering marriage!

I hadn't even begun to heal *any* of my heartaches and pains, and there I was saying "yes" to a marriage proposal. I was hard-headed; I thought I could handle it. Yet, I essentially bought myself a one-way ticket to a living hell because I did not love myself enough to say "no!"

Within a few months into 2000, things had gotten so bad, that I called off the wedding that I had hastily scheduled for September. I left my job at my high school and moved to Elizabeth City State University to take a position as the Assistant Women's Basketball Coach. Although we postponed the ceremony, we remained engaged. I remember knowing that our relationship was volatile, however, I still had hope that we would grow together and mature into marriage material for each other.

My life was comfortable this way until the day I sent a forwarded email to several random friends in my contacts list. It was November, and my University job was Resident Assistant in the very dorm I had lived in

Divorced...NOT Devastated

during my freshman year at Elizabeth City State University. Sitting at the desk at around 11:00 AM, I had mail!

"OH MY GOODNESS! Thank God you contacted me. I have been thinking about you and wondering how you were doing...- Que"

I thought that Quincy and I needed to get together and talk about things face-to-face. It never happened. One day, I ran into one of his relatives who thought fondly of me, but seemingly was not so fond of his current girlfriend. We chatted for a few minutes about Quincy and his parents, and how great we seemed to be together. Unfortunately, near the end of our short conversation, she uttered one sentence that rocked my soul: "Yeah, the baby is due next month." Pause. Drink. Wait. What?

I was broken into pieces. Quincy gave me a weak excuse for not having told me. My heart nearly bled out and again, my hopes were dashed. So, I immediately declared that my wedding was back on! I called all of my bridesmaids and told Marcus to get his guys ready; because we were getting married in August!

By May, things had been rolling along, and I heard from Quincy again. He asked if we could meet to talk that Saturday night while he was in town. Curious, I agreed.

We sat in his SUV near the river. I took a glance into the backseat and stared briefly at the car seat facing me. *That was supposed to be OUR baby.* He apologized again for keeping the news about his son from me and asked me for another chance. I looked over at him, fighting back my tears and I said, "Quincy, what do you want?" He extended his hand, reaching for mine and looked deeply into my eyes. "I want this here. I want us."

Unable to believe what I was hearing, I looked into the back seat again and back at him. I tried to process but was coming up empty. *How in the world is he going to be with me still living there with a NEW BABY!?* I looked him squarely in the eyes and said, "Quincy, I'm getting married. I got out of his vehicle, walked back to mine, and cried all the way home. Everyone tried to talk me out of it. I would not listen.

The night of my wedding rehearsal, I was a nervous wreck. Everyone was in place and the flowers and decorations had been set up. I couldn't believe that I was finally joining the ranks of some of my closest friends who had already taken the plunge. At the same time, I could not believe I was getting ready to follow through with the wedding. Marcus's mother had spent lots of money on various facets of the reception, and my family had secured the catering. Marcus's cousin had made an elaborate wedding cake for us, and all of the wedding party had come from miles away for our special day.

One of my aunts noticed that I was near fainting after we practiced coming into the sanctuary a few times. "Joan, what's wrong with you?" "Auntie, I'm nervous," I said, begging her with my eyes to signal a TKO to everybody so we could just go home.

Divorced...NOT Devastated

"Well, you shouldn't be nervous the night before your wedding. You should be happy and excited. If you're *that* nervous, maybe it means you shouldn't do it." She pursed her lips together and smiled gently. I looked back at her and then down to the floor with nothing to say.

The next day I stood at the altar, happy about the occasion but knowing it was all kinds of wrong. Not because I didn't love Marcus, but because our relationship was based on booze and broken heartedness. I was half-thinking that we were young, and when we officially exchanged rings, we'd get it together. Just before the vows I couldn't shed the thought that we were possibly making the biggest mistake of our lives.

I even glanced over my shoulder after the pastor asked if anyone objected. I wished in my heart that as in the TV sitcom- *A Different World,* Quincy would burst into the sanctuary like Dwayne Wayne did to stop Whitley from getting married, and yell "Joan, NO! Baby WAIT."

I even envisioned his mom as Diahann Carroll, standing and shouting to Quincy, "Die! Just Die!" I guess Quincy did that back in May – with the baby seat in the rear, and I did exactly what I said I would do. I got married and I was pregnant by the end of the month.

By October I was searching online for information about annulment in North Carolina. Marcus would often say that I was bought and paid for, and I suppose that was the prelude for him to make me into what he wanted me to be – a barefoot and pregnant servant, perfectly suited to make him feel and seem like THE MAN. I gave my best efforts

Divorced...NOT Devastated

to be the June Cleaver type of wife he so readily complained to his family and friends about not having. I had never been that way and I couldn't understand why he was bullying me into being something that I wasn't. It all made me feel so inclined to warn Quincy that if he was having problems in his relationship, that they would magnify tenfold in marriage.

On a December night while I was decorating the Christmas tree, the phone rang. The woman on the other end sounded like the consummate telemarketer from somewhere out in the Mid-West. She asked to speak to my husband, and I handed him the phone. After he listened for a few seconds, his face exhibited an expression of disbelief. He handed the phone back to me and drifted out of the front door of the house.

I raised the receiver to my ear. Now the voice had switched from prim and proper, to straight hood. It was Quincy's girlfriend! She had called to say everything you can imagine. She accused Quincy and I of sleeping together and ultimately, that Marcus had better make sure the baby I was carrying was his. She added that "it's probably Quincy's baby."

For the duration of my pregnancy, I endured the slander started by Marcus and his mom that quickly spread around town. I knew I had not done a thing with Quincy, but the accusations and the fact that some crazed lunatic could call us, and her word became gospel made me wish I had. Marcus and I would never be able to recover from that one phone call, and our problems indeed, compounded tenfold, annually, for the next

Divorced...NOT Devastated

ten years! Our daughter came out looking the spitting image of Marcus's mother. *Funny, God. Real funny!*

After a full decade of fighting about money, housekeeping, and always hosting company, it was clear that Marcus and I had been together *too* long. The truth is, Marcus knew back in 1998 that I was vulnerable and not yet over my ex- boyfriend. Additionally, I had not unpacked my childhood baggage and dealt with the carnage it left behind. Simply put, Marcus took advantage, and I allowed him to. I attempted to use him to get over all of the past pain. I went from being an ambitious, sweet young lady, to having all of the self-esteem I had drained from me. By 2011, I was in cognitive behavior therapy, being misdiagnosed and treated for Bipolar Type II Disorder, and passively suicidal.

To win arguments, Marcus often drilled toxicity into me - "Your family doesn't give a shit about you. They know you ain't shit. They've been knowing. That's why they don't call or visit you. But as soon as they *do* call for something, you jump up and run up and down the road behind them!"

Once I was named District Teacher of the Year and Conference Basketball Coach of the Year and honored in the local newspaper for those accomplishments. I got several newspapers and brought them home one day. Just after I spread them out over the coffee table, I sat back to say to myself, "Wow. This feels good!"

Divorced...NOT Devastated

Then like Gargamel, descending onto Smurf Village, Marcus entered the room. It seemed as if he couldn't stand to see me happy or do well at anything. "You can smile all in the paper for being coach of the year and teacher of the year, but you sure ain't wife of the year and mother of the year."

I cried. Often. My friends could expect me to drive up to their home at any given moment; seeking their help as I tried to make sense of what was happening in my marriage. I couldn't believe that the same man who just had to have me, would emotionally gut punch me that way.

What really screamed – *"I don't respect you"*, was the volume of friends that he kept around the house. He worked a swing schedule which amounted to four days off for him at a time. One would think that when two of the guys' marriages ended during this timeframe, that Marcus would get a clue and try to save his! I even tried to have my friends over often. We couldn't keep it up. Some days I hardly had a parking spot in my own yard. Essentially, I felt like a visitor in *their* home.

When I attempted to put my foot down about it, I paid for it. "Joan, this might as well be my house alone. You don't do shit around here anyway!" I did cook and clean – sometimes. It was never enough. I learned that my requests for the boys to find another hangout spot would lead to an argument, or a physical altercation. Therefore, I decided that if I could not beat them, I would join them. Slowly, my quality of life declined, and while I still had dreams; I had very little hope. I stopped believing in love and marriage. I stopped believing in myself and my

Divorced...NOT Devastated

abilities. I was raising my daughter in the blind. My mother had been gone for so long; I could not call upon her for advice. Lacking confidence, I endured years of verbal abuse.

I had finally gotten to the point that I'd say the same prayer to God every night, and I'd curse him each morning that the prayer went unanswered. I wanted to die. Many times, I begged and pleaded not to be awakened the next day, but I would wake up and cry because I was still alive.

I stayed for my daughter. The thought of being alone and dying alone petrified me to the core. After finally giving in one day and telling my therapist just a little about my marriage, she looked me straight in the eye and said, "Goodness! You're not bipolar, you're bi-married!"

I prescription-medicated and self-medicated until I was hanging on by a thread. I don't know how I managed to keep my job. I took sick days here and there because I was drained and overwhelmed. My career was taking a nosedive, and my relationships with family and friends were strained. Hobbies like photography, drawing, coaching basketball, and playing golf were good for me. However, the vodka, arguments, physical violence, and depression exposed my vulnerabilities to the world. Desperately seeking affection, I yielded to extramarital temptations not even limited to the opposite sex. The turmoil that ensued, eventually prompted me to move into the guest bedroom. Needless to say, we were separated on March 14, 2013 in dramatic and volatile fashion.

Divorced...NOT Devastated

I spent the next six months trying to tie up loose ends and save money. I moved out shortly before our first court date to embark on a period of time that was riddled with fear, financial ineptitude, and imposed independence. Again, I cried – often. Joint custody of our daughter has been challenging with the visitation schedule we follow. But she is a remarkable young lady who understands that her mother and father do not belong together.

Today, Marcus refuses to communicate with me, and that's probably the best thing for us, but I monitor how it affects our child. Quincy and I remain good friends and are helpful to each other, both broken from divorce. Moreover, the strength that I found, and the proof God showed me that he'd never fail me, gave me what I was in search of all the while. Peace of mind.

Since the date of separation, my career has taken shape, and each year I've been blessed with some type of promotion. I went on to finally coach a successful basketball season at Bertie High School, finishing 25-2 overall. This time, I was Conference Coach of the Year and District Coach of the Year. Save the insults and hatred! I am now a successful Educational Leader, and I have learned to pay down most of my debts to keep money in my pocket, rather than paying it out just moments after it hits my bank account. The depression is largely gone, and I have finally learned to love myself. Yes, I really love some Joan, and it shows in my self-confidence, energy, and in my smile. I can finally feel love from others and give some, too.

Divorced...NOT Devastated

Divorce began a new chapter in my life called *Divorced Living: The Joan Sharpe Way*. All is well with my soul.

My Takeaways

Never start a new relationship on the rebound. Never. Ever.

You may not think this is important, but it's huge. You can never truly give love to a person whom you've used to clean up the messes from a previous relationship. At the time, it may not even seem to be the case, but after the healing is done, then what? Give yourself an opportunity to shed your old skin and be refreshed for the next relationship.

You must fully love yourself before you can love another.

It's a tall order to ask another human being to be solely responsible for your happiness. This is a hallmark of a codependent relationship. If the two of you are doing well, then you're doing well inside. If your mate is upset with you and you're arguing, then you're dying inside. That's no way to carry on a relationship. Find your inner smile that can sustain its own glow so that your reserves won't be tapped out when you need them most.

You need to identify a list of deal-breakers, or non-negotiables to determine what you will and will not accept from a mate.

We all ignore the things that irritate us during the infatuation phase. That only lasts a short while. Then everything you've ever remotely disliked will become glaring. Just make the list and stick to your guns! You'll thank me later.

Divorced...NOT Devastated

Be honest with yourself and your partner about what you can and cannot deliver.

In short, start out like you can hold out. The representative you send on the first few dates will set you up for failure more times than not.

I have totally forgiven my ex-husband, and most importantly, I've forgiven myself. I was able to do this because God told me,

"I cannot hold you accountable for ending a marriage that I didn't put together in the first place."

Until I find the one He has for me, I will continue to build myself, nurture myself, and most of all, love myself.

Author Ebonie Aiken

Ebonie Aiken

Ebonie Aiken is a public speaker in her field and has obtained an associate degree in Theology and completed four years of coursework toward a B.S in Biology. As a student at the University of North Carolina Greensboro, she became a certified member of the Alpha Phi Omega service fraternity, and from this affiliation, her passion to be an avid volunteer in her community was developed. She later transferred to North Carolina Agricultural and Technical University to continue her studies in Biology.

Today she helps women through her church's women's ministry. Some of the women have been abused or have a history of addiction. Ebonie shares her story to help them understand that, no matter their problems, they can overcome them.

As a mother of two handsome boys, Ethan and Bryson, Ebonie prioritizes and focuses her time on building and nurturing them into great young men of strong character. She is also married to an amazing retired

Divorced...NOT Devastated

Navy Veteran, Christopher Aiken, and they plan to have more children in the near future.

Ebonie often states, that living with Multiple Sclerosis has been, "a blessing in disguise." She explains that now she lives life more fully by appreciating the beauty in the simplicity of everyday life and she now embraces both the ups and the downs. She walks slower due to her condition, which now allows her to "stop and smell the roses". One thing for sure; although she lives with a chronic illness, it has not defeated her!

12 Years A Slave

I want to start my story with one quote that helped me through the worst season of my life. "The WORST thing that could ever happen to you could be the BEST thing for you if you don't let it get the BEST of you". A quote that sums up my story and explains why I am still standing by the grace of God.

At an early age of just four years old, I had a vision and a purpose that God gave me. I knew one part of my destiny and purpose was to be a wife. I was dedicated even then to pray for my future husband because I was raised in the church with my parents and siblings. I would even imagine having to make his plate just like my mother would do for my father. It was purposed in my heart to fulfill my future calling as a wife. My mother would read Proverbs 31 to us weekly to teach us how to be virtuous women. It was my heart's desire and I knew one day my purpose would surely be fulfilled.

As time went on, things began to happen all around me that I was not prepared for. I was naïve and only 19 when I was introduced to a young guy by an acquaintance shortly after my high school sweetheart

Divorced...NOT Devastated

broke up with me. I went from one emotionally abusive relationship just to go right back into another one. And the worst part about it is, I never allowed myself time to heal and grieve. I became a live-in "wifey", cook, sex partner, baby mama and doormat to someone to whom I was not even married. I would do his homework assignments for college and ended up dropping out of college because I could never finish my own.

After my son Bryson was born I thought and prayed that things would be different. But instead, the partying and the cheating just got worse. And my focus was on watching his every move, trying to keep up with the partying and drinking, instead of focusing all my attention on my new born son. He took full advantage of my desire to be loved and my need for something to cover the pain I still had not healed from. I had fallen away from my spiritual upbringing and truly had made a God out of my partner to fulfill the longing in my heart of the child who desired to be a wife.

Every time he cheated I cried my eyes out, but I felt chained to this man. His disrespect went from cheating with my close friends to introducing me to women he was cheating with and saying that they were just friends. I knew the word of God but chose my own path. Exodus 20:5 "You shall have no other gods before me. You shall not make for yourself *an idol* in the form of anything in heaven above or on the earth beneath or in the waters below." God destroys idols. Even good things can become idols, and while reveling and boasting seem good at the time, it is a grave disservice to idolize anything or anybody. The result is God's wrath, on you and the idol. God is a jealous God and *will not be eclipsed.*

Divorced...NOT Devastated

So, at that time, he was driving a Ford Focus and was having car trouble. So, I went to a car dealership to look for a new car for him. He fell in love with the royal blue Escalade. So, we went to the bank to apply for a car loan. The loan was denied with his information, so of course, seeking to please, I went ahead and co-signed. No ring, no true commitment, just believing in a dream that one day I would be a wife.

Shortly after the Escalade purchase, this is about six years in by now, he finally proposed. I thought to myself, "finally, it was all worth it." From the cheating, to the emotional and physical abuse; somewhere in my 25-year-old mind, I just thought, this was the norm.

But shortly after proposing, I noticed he was really not using his Escalade for the transportation needs of our family. Instead, it caused more problems; being a diversion that kept him from home at night. So, I decided to purchase myself a BMW 745 to show him that I too, could stunt. Thinking back now, that was the biggest financial mistake I could have made in my twenties.

One night, he decided he was going to go out and leave me home with our son again. He and I got into a physical altercation and the next day he left, with the Escalade in my name, and moved in with a woman with whom he had been cheating.

At this point, I went into a severe depression. I felt my whole life was crashing before me and that I had hit a brick wall. I was chained mentally to the idea that I had to stay with the father of my son. I kept

Divorced...NOT Devastated

remembering the words of my grandmother saying, "Baby, you've got to marry the one that shot the gun." And I felt like a complete failure. I would call him and apologize over and over, when he was the one who left our family and cheated.

So fast forward a few months, the date that we had set for our wedding finally came, November 7, 2009. But there were no wedding bells or rice to be thrown because he never came back home. That entire day I felt like my heart was being torn in two. Deep inside I was dying a slow death imposed by severe depression.

A few days later, I was in a club celebrating my brother's 21st birthday. I tried to be strong and appear happy, but the entire time all I could think about was suicide.

When I left the club that night, I was driving home with the song "Thank You in Advance" by Boys II Men on repeat. Word for the wise, when you are depressed, do not play love songs when you have a broken heart, instead surround yourself with praise and worship songs.

I was crying to no end and decided to just close my eyes. When I woke up, I was trapped inside of my BMW and it was upside down stuck within a tree. All I could see was the car exploding with me in it. I said to myself, "this is it, this will end the pain." But I looked in the back seat of my car and my son's car seat was there but he was home with my parents. I thought about the pain it would cause him to grow up without his mother. I quoted the words John 3:16 and I made a conscious decision to fight for my life and found a way out through the sunroof, all before the car could explode.

Shortly after that, I was invited to a church called Evangel Fellowship Ministries. I knew God had kept me here for a purpose. Bishop Lockett was the Pastor at the time and I saw a sign on the wall that said, "SUPER SEED NOVEMBER 7, 2010." I saw that it was the same day as my wedding that had never happened, and very clearly, I heard the holy spirit tell me to sow a super seed offering and this would change my life forever.

So, every Thursday night, Sunday morning, and Sunday afternoon I began to attend this ministry and with each service God was slowly changing my heart and healing my pain. This season of my life was truly amazing because it was the start of my first true, intimate relationship with my heavenly father. I began to finally depend on God and became celibate and started fasting and praying because I knew in my heart that something was about to happen that would be an answered prayer and I did not want anything to mess it up.

A few months after being *sold out for Christ*, my ex-fiancé called me and said he had a dream of me in a wedding dress and wanted to give his life to Christ. That was exactly one week after I gave my super seed that he knew nothing about. I just knew in my heart God was answering my prayers. So, my ex-fiancé proposed again, and I said yes.

Divorced...NOT Devastated

We both went on what is known as "The Encounter" which is a three-day face- to- face encounter with God where you leave all your afflictions, pains, and bondages at the cross; because when Jesus died for our sins He did it for every sin, bondage, heartbreak, and pain.

After this happened, on a Thursday night at Evangel Fellowship, I got up in front of the entire church and gave my testimony about how after giving my super seed God had answered my prayers and blessed me with a husband.

Bishop Lockett was so impressed and blessed by my testimony that he agreed to give me a wedding at no cost. The wedding was scheduled a few weeks later, on my birthday, November 27, 2010, to be held in the fellowship hall. I turned twenty-seven on the 27th. Many members of the church came together to help, such as Renae Simon and Ashley Crawley and many others gave of their time and money in support. I just knew it was going to be the start of *happily ever after*.

Shortly after my wedding date, my new husband and I moved to Mebane, North Carolina. I got pregnant with our second son Ethan, a few months after we got married. And suddenly my husband decided to enlist in the military and leave for basic training for six months when I was three months pregnant. So, I was left to fend for our four-year-old son Bryson and our unborn child all on my own.

As the months went by, I continued to go to church, tried to complete my biology degree, and take care of Bryson and the baby on the

Divorced...NOT Devastated

way. I was writing my husband every day. Never in a million years did I imagine my husband was anything but faithful during this time because we had both gone on The Encounter which is true deliverance, and I was pregnant with his son. All the while, little did I know it was a completely different story.

One night when I was at the P.H.D (Prayer, Healing, and Deliverance) Center in Burlington, NC, my family came for prayer for healing for my brother. I was 8 months pregnant. While my brother was being prayed over, I just started shouting and praising God in advance for his healing.

Later that night my water broke while I was sleeping. I woke my four-year-old son Bryson up and he packed all my things while I was calling 911. Since we lived in Mebane and my doctor was in Greensboro, they were unable to send an ambulance to take me to the Women's Hospital in Greensboro.

So, I got my son and I drove myself to the Women's Hospital because no one I knew was close enough to take me there. During the entire 40-minute drive I was just praying, "Lord please let this baby stay inside me." I was so afraid that I would lose him because I was having strong contractions as I drove myself to Greensboro.

By the grace of God, I got to the hospital in time and my doctor went ahead and induced my labor. My dad picked my husband up from basic training. As soon as they arrived my doctor went ahead and

Divorced…NOT Devastated

delivered my little Ethan. However, when she pulled him out there were three loops of the umbilical cord wrapped around his throat and he wasn't crying. I started praying right away and when the doctor unwrapped the cord from my baby's neck, he started breathing and crying. No one, and I mean no one can tell me that God isn't good and faithful to those who love Him! I started crying as I was holding him, and he looked up at me with these innocent eyes of relief. That is why I named him Ethan, which means strong and enduring.

After my son was born and my husband finally returned from military duty, I was so happy to have my family back together again. However, I noticed things had changed with my husband. While we were still going to church together, I noticed he still wanted to go out and party. I became suspicious; so, I went through his phone and discovered that he was having another affair with a girl in the military. I was beyond heart-broken because I thought he had changed and that he was sincere about being faithful in our marriage. I learned in that moment to deal with people according to knowledge. When someone shows you who they are the first time, *please* believe them.

That was my breaking point. I called a mother from our church and she gave me the great advice that finally freed me from the years of slavery I had experienced with this man. I packed my bags and decided to stay with my parents for a few days to see if my husband would change his ways.

Divorced...NOT Devastated

When I returned home, I noticed something was not right about my house. I went to the bathroom and saw a blue toothbrush and then a pink one that was not mine, as well as condoms all over the counter. I saw a pair of pink underwear lying on my bed. And this was the bed that I had constantly prayed over. While we were married, I would literally take anointing oil and sprinkle it all over the bed and pray, "Lord, anoint my bed, make it holy, make it pure; make my intimacy one with him." The same bed that I had spent my last $600 dollars to buy when we first got married. This was the same bed in which I had conceived our son. On top of that, one of my worst fears had happened; he was cheating with a white woman. During our relationship, I always saw him flirt and entertain them. So that was my fear; that he felt I was not good enough for him. I was beyond broken. Indeed, I was a mad, black woman!

When I called my husband to ask him to explain what was going on, he made it clear that the affair wasn't going to end. Brazenly, my husband had moved his mistress into my home and there was nothing I could do about it! So, for almost a week, my children and I were homeless; living out of my car because I did not want to see the hurt and disappointment in the eyes of my parents. One thing for sure, after a few days of sleeping in my car, I realized that there is not that much pride in the world! So, I finally told my parents and they invited us to live with them.

During this low point in my life, I sunk into a deep depression. I questioned how my marriage had failed. How could this have happened? I thought. I prayed, I fasted, I sought the Lord's face. I went to the

Divorced...NOT Devastated

consistently, praying for my husband. But, here I was abandoned; trying to take care of two boys on my own.

I became absent in my kids' life. Each day, I would return from work and just retreat to my room and cry myself to sleep. Broken and depressed, I left the care of my sons to my parents. I know the responsibility of full care of my children and trying to keep me afloat, took a toll on both my mom and my dad. Yet, there was no choice. I was mentally and emotionally depleted.

The day of my divorce was January 27, 2015 and the very next day I was fired from my job. I could not fight back at the time for my belongings. His mistress got the bed I constantly prayed over, and the washer and dryer I had received as a wedding gift from my parents. All I had left was my tv and my kids. And my heart cried out to God, - "Why God, why me? I thought that I was in your will."

I tried to self-medicate to take the pain away, I tried to go out on dates to make it go away, and I even used overeating to make it go away. But the pain remained. Until one day I asked God to please take the pain away, and His response to me was, "Ebonie, I can't take it away, you have to give it to me." I will admit I was angry with God, but I continued to listen for His quiet voice. And God spoke these words to me that would life and give me new understanding of His will. He **ill of God is not meant to please you. The will of** **ut you in a place where you can be used by me,** **ush you into your destiny."**

Divorced...NOT Devastated

Then God showed me the story of Samson. When Samson found himself trusting someone he would allow his heart to be open. Samson was a victim of trusting the wrong people. So many women equate intimacy with trust and we end up falling in love with the wrong person. And that is how I related to the story of Samson: I fell in love with the wrong person.

In the story of Samson, he falls for Delilah who commits the ultimate betrayal. Yet, it is this betrayal and hurt that pushed Samson into his destiny and enables him to fulfill the will of God! The Samson and Delilah relationship had to fail. It was not meant to work. God planted these lessons in my spirit. He was preparing me.

About six months after my divorce, I was driving, and I lost my sight and had an accident. Thankfully no one was hurt, just my front bumper. I called my dad because that was the only name I could make out in my phone. When I went to the hospital, an MRI was ordered, and the results were clear; I had Multiple Sclerosis.

I was lost for words. I was in the hospital for an entire week on steroids. Slowly, my sight came back, by the grace of God. When I was released, my dad fixed the bumper on my car and that day I told my mom I am giving up on the desire to be a wife. My mother looks me in the eyes and said "God surely has not forgotten your super seed and He is faithful to those who believe him; *Trust God*".

Divorced...NOT Devastated

I decided to go out to dinner by myself and finally grieve and accept the fact that I was divorced, with two kids, living with my parents, and now diagnosed with MS.

I went to Brixx because I knew there would not be many people there and I just wanted to be alone. As I sat there the tears began to fall and I asked God, "After everything, Lord, After everything. Now this illness?" As I was wiping the tears from my face, my appetizer came out. But, at that same time, I noticed a handsome man walk into the restaurant.

The waiter sat him three tables down from me, facing towards me. I thought to myself, "it sure would be nice if that man came and joined me for dinner." And then the reality set in, that I was just diagnosed with MS. So I quickly erased that thought out of my mind and looked away. As I was sitting, fiddling with my phone to keep from being nervous, I heard a nice baritone voice say to me, "Do you mind if I join you for dinner tonight?" I looked up and it's the handsome man that walked into the restaurant. I quickly responded with, "why of course" and we sat and had the most wonderful, uplifting conversation I ever had.

I told him I was diagnosed with MS, divorced with two kids, living with my parents and he didn't get up and run off! Instead, he told me to trust God and that he also was living with a rare, chronic illness. He further explained that because he ate healthy and trusted God, he had a clean bill of health. That date was the beginning of the new norm for me. Everyday thereafter, he picked me up and took me out to dinner. He

Divorced...NOT Devastated

joined my church and met my pastor and told him right away that he was dating me with the intent to marry me and that would honor me with celibacy until our wedding night.

I was beyond amazed. I had never met a true man of God that I could introduce to my children and who was willing to join my church and start serving right away. The way he treated my children was something I never thought possible. He began to call them his sons and treated them like Christ would; true agape love.

After four months of dating, he proposed, and I was still in shock that God loved me so much that He allowed me to meet such an amazing, kindhearted, selfless man. One scripture kept ringing in my ears, 1 Cor 2:9 *"Eye has not seen, nor ear heard, nor have entered into the heart of man The things which God has prepared for those who love Him."*

Our wedding date was on May 14, 2016 and now three years later, I still stop and just thank God for orchestrating our connection and allowing us to make a decision that has blessed both of our lives and the lives of our sons forever. I thank God for allowing me to finally experience what true love really feels like. A special thank you to my forever friend, Kimberly Perry- Sanderlin for being a part of our wedding and capturing our most precious moments.

"There is strength in every struggle.
Struggles create opportunities for you
to become stronger, wiser and better.
The moment you shift your thinking
from 'I can not' to 'I must,'
you will begin to see
'Beyond the Pain'
and draw strength from within."

—Kemi Sogunle

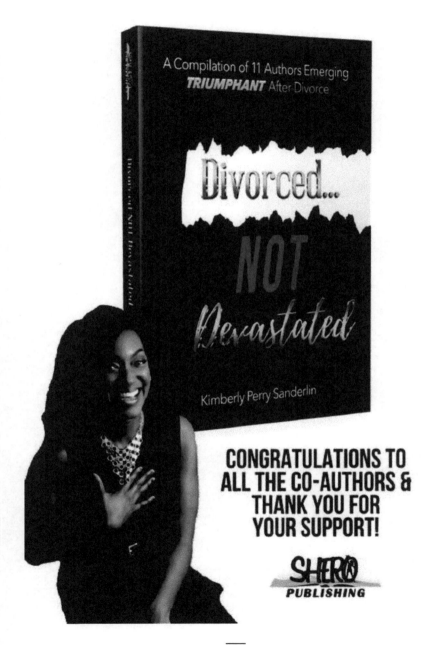